Jeremy & Amy

The extraordinary true story of
one man & his Orang-utan

S
B

First published in 2010 by
Short Books
3A Exmouth House
Pine Street
London EC1R 0JH

This paperback edition published 2011 by Short Books Ltd.

10 9 8 7 6

INSET PICTURE CREDITS
1-12, 21, 25: author's own
13, 15, 16, 17, 18, 19, 20, 26 © Monkey World
22 © L. McCance-Price
27 © S. Bloom

A CIP catalogue record for this book
is available from the British Library.

ISBN 978-1-907595-18-9

Printed and bound by CPI Group (UK) Ltd, Croydon, CR0 4YY

Jeremy & Amy

For Jim... I'll sithee

CONTENTS

PROLOGUE
How to Save a Life

AMY FLITTED BETWEEN my lap and the passenger seat. She was almost a year old by then, a small bundle of wispy red fur with large, quizzical eyes. Sometimes, on our daily trip, she would hang upside down in the rear window, pulling faces at the cars behind her. I am sure it was terribly distracting for the commuters.

We had already been through a lot together and I had been hooked into the world of the orange people – the orang-utans. There was always some sort of innate attraction between me and these magnificent creatures. Chimps are highly intelligent and sociable apes, whose every action is designed to get a reaction; it is easy to listen to them and think World War Three has kicked off. Gorillas, meanwhile, are very gregarious but also a bit thick. I don't mean that nastily. I love them. Perhaps lazy is a better word. They would listen to the chimps screaming blue murder and think, "Oh, I can't be bothered." But the orang-utan is different from both. It is a simple, solitary creature that just wants to eat, sleep, fornicate and work out mechanical formulas. The orang is the grumpy old man of the forest and I suppose I could empathise with that billing. It was why I felt so much for Amy.

There was also the fact that Amy's mother, Jane, had no maternal instincts, which further strengthened our unique bond. When I was a baby and the heating was down in the reptile house at our family zoo, I would share a bed with my mother and a giant python. My mother was blissfully unconcerned about the fact that I was almost exactly the size of the snake's favoured prey. Years later, when Amy was a baby and Jane had discarded her, I kept her warm by borrowing an incubator from the local hospital and force-feeding her every two hours to fend off hypothermia. I knew what it was like to be unwanted as I had also been discarded by my mother and forced to live in a beat-up old caravan at the age of 12, deprived of love and affection. Perhaps that was why I was so drawn to Amy. We were loners.

But then I fell asleep at the wheel on the M2 near Faversham. I was travelling back to my home in Kent with my girlfriend, Meryl, and my son, Jamie. The car climbed the steep banking at high speed and then rolled, nose to tail, back onto the hard shoulder, the impact ripping the roof and shattering the windows. Amy and I suffered head injuries, but Meryl was unscathed and Jamie escaped with a nasty bruise over his kidneys.

By a quirk of fate, one of the first cars to arrive at the crash scene was a police car. Meryl was hysterical. "Help! Help!" she screamed. "There's an orang-utan in the car!" This has all been relayed to me because the next year would be a blur for me. Unlike in the old films, you don't just awake to say, "Where am I?" Consciousness is not like a tap, it's not an on-off situation, and I ended up with a trickle of a half-life.

The two officers surveyed the scene, the woman's ranting about an orang-utan perplexing them. For one of the policemen, Phil, it did worse as he was terrified of all animals. Nevertheless, he got on his hands and knees to examine the wreckage, and realised the roof had collapsed onto the steering wheel. Phil signalled to his partner and then tried to crawl into the mangled wreck from the rear. It was dark and there was a musty smell of animal in the compressed car. Phil dragged his body through the jagged frame of the rear window and saw the back of my blood-soaked head. Trying to assess things, he then noticed a large, hairy hand reach out and wrap itself around the driver's head, cradling it. I had saved Amy. And now she would not let me go.

1

Pan's Garden

THE UGLY TRUTH is that the orang-utan is doomed in
the wild. My view is that they have gone past the point
of no return and they may well never be coming back.
I am biased but I am also a realist. Despite the best
efforts of a lot of very good people, orangs are suffering
because of deforestation, and many of those that are
left are having a terrible life. Some people argue that it
is wrong to keep animals in captivity. It is a debate. But
a lot of conservation is about playing God and deciding which species to save. I have mixed views. I would
do anything for orangs, but I also think that if you
really want to save monkeys, then maybe you should
do it with a breed that has a fighting chance; some-

thing like capuchin monkeys, because they're tough and there are enough of them left. I also think it is terribly conceited to go to Borneo and tell a man who has no other way of making a living and feeding his family that he cannot chop a tree down because you like the monkey up there. It is all a question of survival. I love orangs but I am not playing God. Monkey World is a sanctuary and our job is to rescue individuals. My concern is not saving a species but giving Amy and her son Gordon and the rest a good life. And when I see the photos and evidence coming out of Indonesia, about the horrific things happening there, my con-science is clear because I know I have done my bit.

This book is the story of Amy, an orang-utan who has no right to be alive today, and of me, Jeremy Keeling, the Animal Director of Monkey World. It is also the story of how, together with Jim Cronin, I helped build a 65-acre sanctuary from a derelict pig farm, and how our epic battle for survival is replayed in the wild every single day. On this rollercoaster ride, I will introduce the inhabitants of Monkey World, some of whom will be familiar to you from the *Monkey Life* and *Monkey Business* television series, and a cast of characters including Horace the Tiger, Taffy the Chimp and Harry the Bastard. I also hope to show the great and gossamer ways in which man and beast can co-exist. This is a story of love, hope and survival. And it all started at Pan's Garden.

I was born on October 8, 1956 on a windswept night at the family zoo in the scenic village of Ashover, nestling in the foothills of the Pennines. It is fair to describe us as a dysfunctional family and, by the time I was eight, there were six of us sharing a two-bedroom cottage with seven dogs, a parrot, a chimp, a Senegalese bushbaby, a slow loris, various reptiles and, in a room to itself, a puma. We also had a Himalayan black bear in our outhouse.

Looking back now, it amazes me how dangerous it was to visit our zoo in those days before health and safety was invented. A large number of our enclosures, housing animals such as monkeys, otters, seals and vultures, had no safety barriers to protect visitors from being injured or even maimed. In the event, we were lucky, although the monkeys and parrots developed a notorious reputation for picking the pockets of the more unsuspecting visitor. One day a gentleman arrived at the entrance kiosk in a distressed state and grunting indecipherably. It took quite some time before we realised that one of the mangabey monkeys had stolen his false teeth. Another ambitious primate

stole a lady's wedding ring and was most reluctant to
return it to the hysterical bride, while it only became
clear why the macaw was named Buttons when you
left his company and your clothes fell apart. Just how
he managed to part these objects from their rightful
owners beggars belief.

My mother and father, Jill and Clinton, had an
ambivalent approach to safety. It sounds terrible now
and I shudder at some of the memories, but everything was of its time. Money was tight and it was a
hand-to-mouth existence of cut corners and a stead-
fast pragmatism. That much was evident from the
way they dealt with an early accident.

Pablo the chimp had been rescued from a Spanish
circus, where he had become too big and dangerous
to work. As ever, we were ill-equipped for his arrival,
so we built a makeshift cage in our dining room while
his permanent accommodation was built. I was four
and, by then, we had live-in staff. One young lady's
duties included bathing the owners' children. So one
night she carried me to the downstairs bathroom,
squeezing past Pablo's enclosure. He opened an eye
and was aghast to see his favourite plaything – we
had become good friends – being handled by someone else. Cue an apocalyptic temper tantrum and a

nasty bite to my foot. I was carried to the kitchen table with blood pumping from the wound, while my brother Anthony, whom we all called Pie, mopped the tiled floor. My parents were never ones to burden the health services with our frequent injuries and blood-shedding, but my beloved grandfather, Baba, made me a walking stick and then tried to cheer me up by taking me on a steam train from Matlock to Darley Dale, where the driver blew a steam ring from the funnel in my honour. Most importantly, I retained my friendship with Pablo and, in true chimpanzee style, he had forgotten about the whole affair by the following morning.

I am now astounded at what we managed to get away with through ignorance and naivety. A highly dangerous routine was cleaning the enclosure of Ka-reen, the largest Asiatic brown bear that I have ever met, and her companion, Ursula, our Himalayan black bear. The procedure involved someone stand-ing outside the cage with a jar of watered-down syr-up, feeding the two inmates, while Father entered the enclosure with his shovel and bin. After much pleading, he took me into the cage with him, some-thing he later conceded was extremely foolish, but at the time it was another example of the accepted perils of everyday life.

Many of the events that took place in those early days were barely believable, not only because we all survived them, but also because we were stupid enough to allow them to happen in the first place. A case in point was when the bear enclosure was being concreted to make it safer – an irony in itself – and the animals were being housed temporarily in the goat shed. When the flooring was completed, it was time to return the bears to their new home. That was when Father and his younger brother, Martin, entered the goat shed armed with only a bottle of chloroform and a wad of cotton wool. Their plan was to sedate the bears and somehow manhandle them the 50 yards or so to their cage. I waited outside and listened to the gasps, grunts, bangs and crashes, until the noise abated and the door was flung open to reveal two very groggy bears and two equally dopey men. As was often the case, it was my mother who seized control of the situation and, with the help of Pie and myself, rehoused the bears while the daft duo dozed on a straw bed.

I have always felt that any wild animal is only as dangerous as the person looking after it, and there is no doubt that there was an undercurrent of danger running through the Keeling household. Rebellion coursed through the corridors and there was an internecine conflict between my parents. My mother was the dominant matriarch, her material wealth and breeding ensuring her status. Born lame with a dislocated hip, she compensated with an abrasive attitude. She, too, overcame much, notably the death of her childhood sweetheart in a plane crash just days before they were due to marry. That tragedy forged a strong, intelligent personality with a bitter resentment that she took to her grave.

My father, on the other hand, was a working-class man with delusions of grandeur. He developed a passion for wild animals and set about collecting specimens and learning about their origins. This led to a love of books, and his fondness for the written word was matched only by a total absence of practical aptitude. When my parents met, my mother left my father in no doubt as to his value by telling him firmly that she would never love him.

She was true to her word and we children were divided into warring factions. Pie, Diana and Phoebe were Mother's staunch allies. I was loyal to my father but careful not to side with him overtly. It was not a comfortable place to be. I recall my daddy-loyalty being pushed to the limit one night when my parents were fighting. I intervened but Father pushed me through a window. I remember bleeding with gusto as I watched Mother then brain Father with a poker.

If I can credit them with any parental skills, it was with instilling in me a sense of independence. When I was 11 and Pie was 13, we were effectively left in charge of Pan's Garden. At the time we had a teenage girl living in the large zoo house on the hill and caring for our 200 animals. It had been a gorgeous, baronial place when my grandfather lived there, but had become increasingly run down when our menagerie had replaced him. We had since moved to an old cottage a few miles away in Uppertown, leaving our staff member alone in a house that always made me think of the sinister shack in *Psycho*, the Alfred Hitchcock film.

Unfortunately, a lorry driver who was the brother of a former staff member had developed a severe crush on our teenager and would pester her each night. It got so bad that, in the end, she had a nervous breakdown and was hospitalised. That was when the call came to me at junior school. I was to leave immediately. There was a crisis at home. Pie had the same call at Claycross Secondary Modern, where he was a prisoner.

School was always an unnecessary burden, as far as I was concerned, and so I fled home, pulling on my blazer as I climbed the hill leading to the zoo. On arrival, my mother quickly explained the situation. My parents were too busy on the lecture circuit to look after the animals and so, with our poor staff member in hospital, it was down to us two boys. As a token effort of support, my mother said she would do any required husbandry with the rattlesnake in the reptile house.

In many ways this was a dream and, in truth, the daily routine of feeding and cleaning the chimps, bears, pumas, monkeys, birds, wild dogs and the leopard was second nature. The one problem was that we lived in fear of the return of the frustrated suitor as we were now spending all our time alone in the house on the hill. Mother's basic advice was to tell him that we had no idea where the woman had gone if he showed up. After a week of nightly visits and our protestations of ignorance, the lorry driver became very angry. In fear, we reported back to our mother, pointing out that we could not even lock the door as protection. Her response was phlegmatic.

"If we're going to be burgled I'd rather they did not break the door down," she said. "That'll be another expense."

It was not burglary we were concerned about, rather that we would have to deal with the intruder on our own. My task, then, was to devise a trap that would kill, or at the very least maim, our unwanted visitor. I relished the task and, before long, was winching a bicycle, discarded by our staff member, up above the door, via a pulley system and with a simple trigger mechanism attached. Right on cue, we heard our lorry driver arrive. He barged open the unlocked door and, to Pie's utter disbelief, the trap worked perfectly. The bicycle clattered down onto him from a great height and I congratulated myself for my Heath Robinson-like skills. The only flaw in the plan was that the bike had not actually killed the lorry driver, but merely enraged him further, and he charged at us in a fury. Somehow in the fracas one of us managed to make a call to Mother and the police were called. There ensued a major manhunt for the sinister suitor, who was eventually caught and got six months, while our staff member returned to work. Sad to say, happy endings rarely lasted in the house of horrors.

2
House of Horrors

As I WALK around Monkey World and look at Amy in one of our huge enclosures, I feel relieved at how much progress has been made in looking after wild animals. The backlash against zoos has forced it, which is a good thing, although we have avoided any such negativity because we are a sanctuary. We're the good guys. But even though the facilities and resources have changed beyond all recognition, my underlying love for animals has not changed since the blood, sweat and tears shed back in the house of horrors.

Digger was a dingo. He was usually very passive, but one frosty morning, while cleaning his enclosure, my father slipped and ended up on his back. Instantly

Digger reverted to instinct and went for the throat. Father managed to get his hands across his neck as protection in the nick of time as Digger dug in. Pie and I waded in with brooms and shouts and managed to shepherd Digger away, leaving father lying there, bleeding and ashen. My parents preferred not to bother with trifles such as doctors, but there was no option on this occasion so we took him to the Chesterfield Royal Hospital, where we stuck to our golden rule of never confessing how our injuries had occurred. Fearing negative press or repercussions in the village, we told the doctor that a domestic dog had caused the deep wounds. The doctor looked dubiously at the arm with its serrated bite marks and said, in a broad Australian accent: "Jeez, looks more like a bloody dingo bite to me!"

We kept to our implausible story as his nimble fingers applied the 40 stitches needed to repair Digger's handiwork.

Father could be the perpetrator too. Pie's pride and joy was Cherokee the puma. Her mother, Sioux, showed as few maternal instincts as our own mother did, so the cub was removed and hand-reared. She would never be a prime specimen because Pie could never find the perfect match for puma milk, but she was healthy and happy. She was also still living with us in the over-crowded cottage in Uppertown by the time she was an adult, but one night she made a bid for freedom as Pie and I arrived home from Pan's Garden. I slammed the garden gate shut while Mother covered another potential escape route, but Father was aghast.

"The puma's got out!" he cried. "The puma's escaped!"

As his frenzied cries spiralled into the sky, Pie tried to placate him.

"Don't panic, Father," he shouted. "We have everything under control."

I knew it was a mistake as soon as the words were out. Affronted by Pie's words, Father said, "Panic? Me? Panic?"

Thereupon, he picked up Pie by the scruff of his neck and hurled him across the dining room onto Mother's prized sofa. The four legs snapped simultaneously, leaving Pie entangled on the floor. Meanwhile, I ushered Cherokee back to the sanctuary of her room, fully understanding why she might want to flee from this place.

I hate the word expert but I like the word expertise. That's what it comes down to when dealing with dangerous animals. There have been lots of occasions when keepers have pushed it too far and reaped the awful consequences. The relationship can fall apart at any moment, even with an animal I have known for as long as Amy, and you can never lose sight of that. People talk about how strong animals are, whether they be orang-utans or tigers or dingoes, but really it is we humans who are proportionately so weak. Hence, it is a matter of respect.

I might have wondered at my mother's balancing of expertise and respect when one of our allies, John Foden, the curator at Drayton Manor Zoo, said we could have a banded krait. This particular snake is so venomous that no known serum exists to counter its bite. Indeed, it has been reported that a bullock died within 30 minutes of being bitten by one. John was one of the world's leading experts on venomous reptiles, but placed the krait in an old pillowcase for the journey from Drayton Manor. Mother picked up the pillowcase and placed it in her rickety old Ford Popular. She was halfway into the 80-mile journey when she felt something moving against her skin. The snake had located a hole in the pillowcase and was seeking warmth in a hostile environment. Unfazed by her new use as a radiator for a potentially lethal animal, Mother pulled over, parked the car and calmly placed her uninvited guest back in the pillowcase, no doubt telling him what a naughty boy he had been as she tied a piece of string around the hole.

Whether I learnt much of any use from such prosaic methods is debatable, but I certainly learnt more from them than I did at school. Everyone was dumbstruck then, when my headteacher at junior school addressed us all at assembly one day. "We have a surprise to announce this morning: one of our pupils has passed the 11 plus and won a scholarship to an exceptional school in Chesterfield called William Rhodes," he intoned. "And you will be amazed to hear that the student's name is… Jeremy Keeling."

Amazement swiftly faded to disappointment. I was disruptive at William Rhodes, where I was surrounded by boys from middle-class backgrounds, and quickly became an apathetic and periodic presence. "It's a shame Jeremy is not encouraged to become a full-time member of this establishment," my school report stated one year. "Impossible to assess owing to absences," lamented the next.

My mother felt I had more important matters to attend to and, for once, sided with me. Bristling after a reprimand for not providing an explanatory note for each absence, she telephoned the headteacher,

Mr Crookes, and said, "I have far better things to do than write letters to you. If Jeremy is absent then it is with my full consent."

By the time I left school, Mr Crookes had long washed his hands of me. I stood in front of him on my last day as he signed my parole – at least that's how I viewed it – and listened to his verdict. "I despair of you, Keeling," he said. "You will never make anything of your life." Nevertheless, he was as glad as I was to be scribbling his name on my leaving certificate.

My parents finally separated in 1970. Father's lectures took him all over the country and he would scrounge a bed for the night from his associates. One of these was an old lion-tamer friend who had started a relationship with a beautiful and wealthy divorcee. Together they had started up a zoo in the grounds of her large property. It was not long before the lion tamer was replaced by my father, which seemed to me a very poor way to treat a friend.

I had become fascinated by all things mechanical in my early teens and helped repair cars for pocket money. I also worked for a local farmer, haymaking and milking cows, although payment was erratic, it must be said. I had no self-esteem at all. When I got hold of an old James motorbike from a scrap heap, I was thrilled and showed it to my father, craving some approval.

"Did you hear that?" I said as I revved the engine.

"It pains me to listen," he responded wearily.

Father never did foster any enthusiasm in his children and, when he left, the outbreak of peace was a huge relief.

One man who did notice and fuel my interest in repairing and constructing cars was Bill Barker, a talented engineer who ran the nearby Peglant Garage. When delivering a car to my mother one day, he saw my feet protruding from beneath a dilapidated vehicle perched on an equally suspect jack. On the way out, having sold my mother one of Barker's bangers, as I would refer to them, he saw my feet still in place and told my mother he could use me. And so I began work with Bill and he taught me the secrets of car repair and welding, things that have been of great use to me ever since. We worked hard on restoring insurance write-offs and building beach buggies and trailers, turning our hands to anything that was within our means, and became a good team.

Sadly, Barker's garage was a shed with no toilet or running water and, now that the Factories Act had come in, Bill could not legally employ anyone. He paid me a miserly £1 a day, but Bill did ensure I attended Chesterfield Technical College on day release, where I came top in my year.

Father's absence had repercussions and, though we briefly lived in an oasis of calm, we struggled financially. Running the zoo had always been a struggle, a labour of love and hate, and now it was impossible. With only one meagre income from my mother's occasional lecturing to support us, we made our staccato journey towards the inevitable. It was the survival of the fittest and Pan's Garden could not keep pace.

Luckily, we managed to rehome almost all of our animals, many at Father's new enterprise with his rich divorcee. Resources were tight for everyone, but one man agreed to take our two bears. It was the end of an era, as Ursula had lived in our outhouse since we were small and had grown up with us. It was with mixed feelings that I greeted the man from Essex who was to take our bears to his collection. We had already placed Ursula in a sturdy crate and in the van, and then moved on to Kareen, the brown bear. She went into a rather flimsier temporary crate and we left her there while we broke for a coffee. As we walked away, there was a loud crashing noise. We turned to see Kareen standing amid a pile of broken timber. She had simply flexed her considerable muscles, and our carefully constructed travelling crate was now a pile of matchwood. The man from Essex could not wait. This was a one-time offer only. He went away with Ursula and we were left with Kareen. We had tried every available avenue. Every stone had been turned. There was no way out. I was distraught when I realised the dreadful consequences. Later that day, Kareen was shot by a local marksman. The horror and sadness of that day have never left me. The same fate met our wild boar, Baron Herr Von Routeler, or Rooty to his mates. I am not an overly sentimental man, but losing an animal is a terrible experience. Perhaps we were lucky that, of all our 400 or so animals, only two met this fate, but I nevertheless class it as one of the worst days of my life.

Our tempestuous home life continued when Father tried to make contact with his children. We agreed to meet and a date was set when my mother would be absent. Father had a habit of squeezing the maximum amount of drama out of every situation. Hence, we assembled before him in the cottage in a row, like errant schoolchildren in front of the headmaster. Father gave a Churchillian speech from the heart, pleading for our support, but his words fell on deaf ears as far as my siblings were concerned, as they were truly loyal to the mother camp.

I alone said that I would not mind if he wanted to keep in touch and visit from time to time. "Yes, of course," I said, little knowing the consequences I would suffer from that simple betrayal. I became exiled from the rest of the clan through my love of a peaceful life. I was all too aware of my father's manifold shortcomings, but I also felt sorry for him and felt some strange, twisted sense of loyalty. Father was pleased to have enlisted one recruit and packed up some books with a smile on his face. I later appreciated that the books had been the primary reason for his visit. He put the box in the back of his car and drove back to his new zoo, leaving the usual human detritus in his wake.

The relationship between the parent and offspring varies wildly from species to species. If you come to Monkey World, you might see an orang mother like Hsiao-quai cuddling her baby in a manner familiar to humans. The flipside is infanticide and the discarding of runts. Some orangs form strong bonds; others have no maternal instincts. This can seem shocking to us, but is it any less cruel than the drip-feed of discontent and emotional warfare that often plagues human households?

I did retain contact with my absent father and even visited him on occasion. These clandestine missions were carried out with the help of Pie. One day the two of us set off to meet Father at a motorway service station on the way to Cambridge. Pie was driving our ageing Morris Minor van, but negotiating the right of way at a roundabout just outside Mansfield, there was a misunderstanding and, suffice it to say, we lost. I looked to my left just in time to see a bright yellow Post Office van crash into the side where I was sitting.

I drifted in and out of consciousness as Pie hauled me from the car. He was equally disorientated and scared. He told me to go and find a phone box to ring Mother. Even in my condition, dazed and confused, I knew that idea was a double-edged sword and that she would be furious to hear I had been sneaking off to see her lesser half.

I passed out on the pavement and the next thing I knew I was in the prone position in the back of an ambulance. They seemed to know what they were doing and the ambulance was cosy compared to the Morris Minor. I sank back onto the bed and went to hospital to get my wounds mended.

Unbeknown to me, Pie was oblivious to my departure in the ambulance and, when my mother arrived, the pair spent several hours combing the streets, looking for me. Eventually, they considered looking at the local hospitals. I vividly recall my mother limping along the corridor with piratical menace and confronting a doctor.

"This is all very inconvenient," she reprimanded him.

Pie, meanwhile, decided to go and watch a football match in Chesterfield, leaving me concussed, confused and alone in a hospital bed. Father was informed of the problems, but rather than come and see me, turned back and trundled home to his zoo. Mother discharged me the next morning.

"It's totally unnecessary you being here," she said.

"They say I have concussion," I ventured.

"Nonsense."

Worse was to follow. My mother struggled to come to terms with what she deemed an act of treason on my part in attempting to see my father. So when I was 12, she banned me from the house.

"You're a boorish, ill-mannered lout, just like your father," she said.

So I began living in a beat-up caravan in one of the back fields, paying my mother £4 a week for the privilege. Out of sight and mind. I worked evenings and weekends so I could eat and then, each Friday evening after school, I would visit the launderette in Chesterfield, where I would undress and wash my uniform. I took to begging on the streets and lived off free school meals. And beneath it all was a dark secret that I would keep locked away for almost four decades.

I began working for Bill on a full-time basis and took solace in the mechanical world. One thing my mother had given me was total freedom when it came to cars. In fact, I was still at junior school when she allowed me to drive the family vehicle. This attitude was born of practical needs. Indeed, necessity really was the mother of invention. We lived an isolated existence and so transport was a lifeline. If I could drive then I could help. Never mind the legality of such matters. I was so desperate to have my freedom and a potential escape route that I applied to take my driving test at the first available opportunity on my 17th birthday. And when I finally shed those L-plates, it was a milestone reached and a millstone lifted from around my neck.

Alas, my driving skills were the source of much debate. Pie would forever lament my boy-racer tendencies and we had bets over whether I would manage to kill myself before anyone else did. These remarks were made half in jest, but they would come back and haunt me in a terrible fashion a decade later.

Bill sold his business and, thanks to a good friend called Colin Ainsworth, I started working at another garage, Taylor's, repairing farm vehicles. I had no idea where I was going in life but wherever it was, I was carrying a lot of baggage. I could certainly never have guessed that the journey would somehow lead me to being involved in rescue missions and forging an unbreakable bond with a large, cantankerous orang-utan. I was stuck and so the only thing to do was flee.

I knew where I was going when I turned up for our usual Thursday evening lads' night at The Red Lion in Ashover, however. We decided to finish the night back at my caravan, so half a dozen of us piled into a couple of cars and we began the short trip. I was driving the lead vehicle and had just rounded a tight bend when I saw a curious-looking creature standing in the middle of the road, his eyes flashing in my headlights. He scampered off to the right and darted up a tree. I slammed on the brakes and got out. I knew that this was Mr Possum, an animal that had escaped from Pan's Garden many months before and was assumed lost for ever. Now, it was clear that the resourceful possum had in fact been living the life of Riley in the wild.

I began to climb the tree after him, glad that I had not overindulged in the pub. I saw him shrinking away ahead of me, but finally he ran out of tree. I clung to the trunk and thrust out my arm along the branch. I managed to grab his tail and pulled him towards me. Then I got hold of him around the neck, to prevent him biting me, although he did manage to slash my thigh during the skirmish. It was only then that I looked down to witness a sea of bewildered faces standing below me.

"Can someone drive to my mother's and get a box for him?" I shouted.

There was a rumbling and sniggering, but a car drove off towards the house of horrors. My friends had seen nothing yet. Ten minutes or so later, I saw the wink of headlights meandering down the tree-lined lane. Then Mother opened the door. My friends were shocked to see her clamber out of her wilting old van, wearing a dressing gown tied loosely together with some bale string. Shock turned to horror when Mother removed her dressing gown and, with the help of a few others, used it as a safety net for her beloved possum as we descended. Mother then placed him in the travelling box and left, dressed only in a flimsy nightdress, as if nothing untoward had happened at all. If I needed convincing, that moment was the deciding factor. I had to get out.

3

Escape

IN THE WILD, an animal, such as an orang-utan, is let
go from the family unit only when it is independent.
You could argue that I had yet to reach that level of
maturity when I took off, but it was a small step on
a road that would take me across the globe and allow
me to indulge my passion for animals. Yet, back then,
with the family splintering after years of bickering and
physical abuse, it was me that needed rescuing. And
there is no doubt that the orang-utans helped.

My experiences had turned me into a bitter, anti-
social young man with a festering resentment that
bubbled perilously close to the surface. It was my time
to rebel and I seriously thought about turning to a life

of crime. Father's contact had dwindled to nothing and he had fled his new zoo after a horrible tragedy in which his lover's young son was killed when trapped in the door of a school bus. Another zoo failed in his absence and the animals were sold on. Father made an ill-fated attempt to return to my mother, but she was incredulous at his sheer gall and he disappeared once again, leading nature trek expeditions to Canada and Iceland.

To his dying day, he would tell anyone about how he was thrown out of his magical zoological garden by my wicked mother. While I would never defend my mother, it never ceases to amaze me how people rewrite history to fit their favoured version.

Pie took a job at Brighton Aquarium and then at Cricket St Thomas Zoo in Somerset. My sisters, Diana and Phoebe, stayed with Mother, who was contemplating leaving Derbyshire herself, to start a lecturing service. It was one day around this time that Diana went to the school doctor and was informed that she was about to give birth. Alan arrived a day later. Diana was 13. I felt ashamed because I had made numerous jibes about Diana's weight gain, likening her to a beached whale and never imagining the true cause.

I headed off to Sussex in an elderly Mini Cooper

and found lodgings in a run-down bedsit close to the sea in Worthing. I got a job repairing lorries for a mushroom-growing company and was a frequent visitor to Granny, who lived a few miles away and prided herself on feeding all who entered. The grass is not always greener though and I soon had itchy feet again.

I traded in my Mini for a Ford Cortina and came across a stray old English sheepdog whom I named Scruffy. I did not know where I was going or what I was looking for, but in the spring of 1974 I loaded all my possessions into the car and went walkabout. It was a six-month lost weekend as Scruffy and I bummed around England in search of something better. Poor old Scruffy was a fine travelling companion and I can only thank him for his friendship and patience. It may have been fortunate for him that his breed is possibly not the most intelligent and, hence, hopefully, I did not bore him too much. Curiously, I cannot recall much about this period. It is just a blur, as if someone had pressed a pause button while things fell into shape. All I remember is that I made a point of not visiting anyone that I had ever met and that I slept rough the whole time. It was as if I was trying to purge myself of an unhappy past and the years of abuse, but the result was that I stunk to high heaven.

One night I stood on the North Yorkshire Moors with Scruffy. Everything was reduced to a green canvas. All sounds softened to a warm monotone. I could think of no safer place to be than standing up there alone, knowing that there was not a human being in sight for several miles. Those wanderlust urges have never left me and neither has the value of isolation.

Eventually, my timeout was over and I knew I had to return to the real world. I knew where to go, too. Ever since I had been a baby, Molly Badham and Nat Evans had been firm family friends. These two ladies would become famous for building up Twycross Zoo, but we knew them when they were located in their very first zoo, Hints, near Tamworth. That had been the scene of my first animal-related accident while guzzling a bottle of milk in a pram. One of the resident chimps took exception to seeing so much food disappear down my throat and grabbed my bottle. I refused to release it, whereupon the chimp inevitably sank his teeth into my foot. The chimp disappeared up the tree with my lunch, while I bled profusely and Mother tried to silence me with some more food.

I knew that Molly and Nat were often on the lookout for staff and so I called in to offer my services. These two marvellous women greeted me with open arms. We discussed the case of the lost lunch and, as it emerged that they were indeed suffering a staffing crisis, they employed me on the spot. It was Bonfire Night and I felt a flicker of a flame inside me. For all the mayhem, misery and mischief, there was something reassuring about being back in close proximity to animals again.

I rehoused Scruffy with a very nice couple in Leicestershire and was looking forward to my new role. Unfortunately, it did not quite match the picture I had painted in my mind. I used my last penny on petrol to get to Twycross and was directed to my quarters. Imagine my horror when all I found was a decrepit caravan with an empty gas container in the corner. I asked Molly about the lack of gas, as the winter was already biting like a hungry chimp.

"You can buy a new one when you get your first wage," she said.

Molly also instructed me to get my chest-length hair shorn off and gave me 20 pence and directions to the barber. I dutifully submitted and felt like Samson as I watched great clumps of hair fall around me. Molly was unimpressed with the result, though, and told me to go back and request the regulation short back and sides.

That night, frozen and hungry, I began to wonder what sort of hell I had let myself in for. I thought I was doing these people a favour because they were so short-staffed, but I felt like a prisoner again. Living in a caravan once more.

The next day passed uneventfully and I was thrilled to be back in the presence of so many chimps. I realised how much I had missed them. Chimps are such interesting, active animals. They are always vying for position and needing stimulation, so a new keeper was a source of great amusement to them. However, as night closed in, my heart sank into my threadbare boots at the thought of returning to the caravan with no heating, light or food. So, before I knew it, I was packing again. Running away seemed my best option. Had I been older and wiser, I would have explained things to Molly, but I was not. And so, to my eternal regret, I fled under the cloak of darkness, sneaking off without informing Molly and Nat of my predicament. It was a cowardly act that I have been ashamed of ever since.

I drove to Whitwick, where two friends of Pan's Garden, Tony and Dorothy Walker, lived. They gave me a cooked meal and a warm bed for the night and I felt like I was in heaven. I stayed for a few days, earning enough loose change to buy some petrol and a packet of cigarettes, and was then off again.

The next stop on this nomadic trail was Colchester Zoo, which was run by another family friend, Frank Farrah, a small, self-made northerner with a considerable talent for animal husbandry. He too had a chronic staff problem. Frank was able to offer me accommodation with the café manager, who lived in a council house overlooking the local army barracks, in return for looking after his primate collection. I snapped his hand off at the chance.

It was here that I gained my introduction to the orange people, as I would rechristen the orang-utans, and I suppose this was my epiphany. I was 18 and I was responsible for chimps, drills, baboons, spider monkeys, capuchins, mangabeys, guenons, gibbons and lemurs, but the main draw for me were Guy and Prissy, the zoo's two orang-utans.

They are, of course, great to look at, but I think it was their solitary lifestyle that really appealed to me. You just get on better with some people than others and it is exactly the same with animals. I'm not a naturally gregarious person and the orangs' independent streak drew me in. Maybe I saw myself in them. The male orang is very much the grumpy old git. A chimp will want to interact and play, but an orang will look at you as if to say, "Sod off, I'm busy." I could understand that. "I'm not bothered with your social niceties. Now get lost!" Even after all these years, with Amy a veteran of Monkey World and her mother, Jane, well into her fifties over in San Diego, the appeal has not dimmed. I am not sure why, but the fact is these creatures hold me in awe and admiration every time I am in their presence.

Frank had a novel approach to running his zoo. One day I was cleaning under the chimps' cage door, when one of them snatched my dustpan. I studied the situation and wondered how I could get the pan back, as this group of sub-adult males was not about to hand over its trophy. At that very moment Frank appeared. He assessed the state of play in a nanosecond, flung open the door and slapped the bemused thief over the head affectionately. He then picked up the dustpan and handed it back to me. "There you go, love," he said.

On another day I watched as a massive red kangaroo kicked Frank clean over a fence. The matter-of-fact manner in which he picked himself up and dusted himself down made him rise even higher in my estimation. I learnt much from him, even how to crate a large male ostrich in the dead of night with only a length of hosepipe. The adrenaline rush I felt as I went home that night was akin to that of a prizefighter after his greatest conquest.

The orangs could be awkward too. One day we were having our lunch when a member of the public rushed in. He was dragging his family behind him and his eyes were as wide as saucers. "Come quick!" he yelled. "One of your monkeys has escaped." I sipped my tea and sighed. One of our monkeys had recently had a baby, which was so small that it would sometimes climb through the gaps in the cage. These escapes lasted only for a few minutes and the baby would always be pulled back inside, so it was not a great concern.

"Don't worry," I told him. "It happens all the time. She'll go back soon."

The man looked dumbfounded. "All the time?" he repeated slowly.

"Yes. It's not ideal, I know, but it's really nothing to worry about."

"Er, are you sure?"

"Absolutely."

"I still think you might want to come and take a look."

I realised the man was not going to be placated and

so, to humour him, I downed my tea and followed him out of the dining room. That was when I saw the crowd and realised something was not quite right. I brushed through the bodies and, to my horror, saw Prissy, one of the orangs, sitting proudly on top of her enclosure. With the help of Guy, she had found a way of escaping and was relishing the attention. I suddenly understood why the man had been so bemused by my ambivalence. Some time later, using a bag of old paper as a carrot – Prissy loved tearing up paper – I coaxed her down and back inside. She was a good-natured thing and it was not as though the public was in any danger, but it was scarcely ideal. I left her to her shredding and breathed a sigh of relief.

My dealings with the staff at Colchester were mixed, but I later realised I was still exuding an air of menace in those days of teenage rebellion. I was something of a brawler at school, and was regarded as the cock of the first, second and third years. Then a very good friend of mine named Donovan Spencer, the sole Jamaican lad in the school, put me in my place. I have been a pacifist ever since and never thought twice about why Eddy the elephant keeper took his lunch in the disused railway dining car with a large spanner on the table in front of him. It was some time before it was pointed out to me that Eddy was scared of me and felt he needed protection lest I launch an unprovoked attack.

I was distressed to hear that, but had made friends with another keeper named Stewart J Irvine, an American who had just graduated from the University of Utah with a zoology degree. However, one casual comment from him stuck in my mind as I think it represents the attitude of many in our profession.

"Jeez," he lamented. "I'm no more than a glorified lavatory attendant."

I could not help thinking then, as I have of many other people since, that he had chosen the wrong career.

My closest relationship was with Gill, who cared for the nocturnal animals and aquarium. Our paths crossed as we went about our daily routines and, even though she was 30, some 12 years older than me, I found her company to be a great comfort. Her fierce independence gelled with my abhorrence of sharing. The match was an instant success.

Gill was in debt. She had been on an animal-collecting trip to South America, à la David Attenborough and Gerald Durrell, but the trip had failed and Gill had been left stranded. The costs of getting home had been enormous and she was now struggling with the bills. The frequent visits to Pan's Garden by the bailiffs had left me afraid, indeed terrified, of any form of debt. And so, as we became a couple, I quit working at the zoo and we moved to Bishop's Stortford where I found work reconditioning engines in a factory, while Gill worked as a housekeeper in return for lodgings.

Before long the slate was wiped clean and I wiped my brow. Two months after meeting, Gill and I were married at Bishop's Stortford register office. The factory job had been a means to clearing the debt before we embarked on married life, and I was ready to return to working with animals. In fact, I craved it. Every week I scoured the back pages of *Cage & Aviary Birds*, the only magazine used by zoos to advertise jobs. It was a largely fruitless exercise and I began to despair. But then, one day, I came across a small box ad for a keeper to look after a private collection of apes and big cats in Weybridge. I tore out the advert and stuck it in my pocket. Little did I know that I would soon be living in a mansion and taking tigers for tea with pop stars. I was about to become the rock 'n' roll zookeeper.

4

The Rock 'n' Roll Zookeeper

GORDON MILLS WAS a multi-millionaire music impresario and tax exile living in America. He had been a talented songwriter, penning hits for Cliff Richard and Johnny Kidd and the Pirates, but had struck gold by taking Tom Jones, Engelbert Humperdinck and Gilbert O'Sullivan to mega-stardom. Now he owned a lavish estate called Little Rhondda, an homage to his Welsh roots, in St George's Hill, the country's first gated community and home to the likes of John Lennon. It was also home to what would become the largest private zoo in the world.

I waltzed through my interview. The man asking

the questions was the head keeper. He was a rather lazy man, in my view, and must have regarded my teenage enthusiasm as manna from heaven. With Gordon spending most of his time in the States, he was free to take it easy, hidden away among the Scots pine while his paymaster was away making money. This apathetic figure clearly felt I was too callow a youth to blow his cover and, thus, he could get me to do the dirty work.

I scarcely cared. I was looking after eight gorillas, three orang-utans, six tigers and one puma in a collection that was not open to the public. To make this scenario even better, Gordon was rarely in residence and happy to delegate to the pros. Gill and I were given a bungalow, recently vacated by Gilbert O'Sullivan, the Irish piano-playing singer who had become a huge star and had moved on to bigger and better things. A year later, Jamie, my first son, arrived, after a 29-hour labour. It was the hottest summer for years, which did not help Gill's mood much. The good news for me was that the lengthy labour gave me enough time to get home and feed and clean the chaps before returning to see the action. I was still little more than a boy myself, really, but enjoyed being a father and was determined to be a better parent than mine had been to me. Suddenly, everything had changed, and when I thought back to begging and sleeping rough and shivering in the un-heated caravan at Twycross, I could hardly believe my luck.

Gordon cared for his animals but there is no doubt he was doing this partly for his ego. He knew John Aspinall, the bookmaker turned Mayfair club owner who had his own collection at Howletts, his Kent mansion, bankrolled by the success of his gambling empire. At that time Howletts was not open to the public either, but it would go on to play a pivotal part in my life. It would also become well known for its encouragement of close relationships between man and beast, occasionally leading to fatal misjudgements. But back in 1974, Gordon and John Aspinall were friendly rivals who had watched gorillas together in the Congo. This was the era of the private menagerie. It was a status symbol to rank alongside the gold Rolls-Royce Corniche that Gordon let me drive while he was away.

Within a month of starting to work for Gordon, one of the Bengal tigers gave birth to five cubs. That was a large litter for a female tiger to cope with, and so it was decided that two of the cubs should be removed and hand-reared. My co-worker took these home, and Peter and Lady, as they became known, soon got used to the old-fashioned diet of diluted Carnation milk. However, one of the surviving cubs was struggling and would spend its days lying face down, legs splayed, almost like a tiger-skin rug.

We had no option but to take Horace from his mother, Rhanee, and make a trip to London Zoo's veterinary hospital, where it was discovered that the young chap had a rare genetic disorder that left him with this hopeless "swimming" posture. The man at London Zoo shook his head.

"There's a five per cent chance of survival," he said in a scientific voice bleached of emotion. "I suggest euthanasia."

With such a gloomy prognosis, my co-worker was happy to hand Horace over to me, and so my first rescue mission began in earnest. I was damned if I was going to have him put to sleep. That attitude stemmed from my time at Pan's Garden, when euthanasia was the very last resort. It was the culture I came from, if you can call it a culture, and so I worked out a plan.

In the first few weeks of life, mobility is not a problem for a newborn cub, but it quickly becomes more needy and active. Luckily, I had hit on a winning formula. I had done my research and found a milk substitute that was specially manufactured for cats. It, therefore, had a much better nutritional value than the evaporated milk being used for Peter and Lady, but my co-worker took any of my suggestions as precocious interference. He had worked at Chipperfield's Circus and Carnation milk worked there, so understandably his attitude was "if it ain't broke, don't fix it". However, my way proved the better as Horace soon began to thrive, whereas Peter and Lady lost all their fur.

The main problem I had with weaning Horace was a common one when hand-rearing tigers. All mammals suckle and so they need a nipple. Hence, a baby's bottle is a good replacement. With tiny marmoset babies I have used pipettes as they are the size of the mother's teat. Tigers start to get their teeth very quickly so one day, as I cradled Horace and gave him his bottle, milk began to spray everywhere as if from a broken fire hydrant. Horace, I quickly realised, had bitten into the nipple. That was when I knew it was time for him to start drinking from a bowl.

The trials and tribulations of Horace meant I did have some contact with Gordon in those early days. His wife, Jo, who had been a runner-up in Miss South Africa before embarking on a successful career as a model and co-writing such songs as "It's Not Unusual" with her husband, still lived at Little Rhondda with their kids. She did not want to take them to America, although she would give in and follow Gordon within a few months. I was glad she was there, though, because she was a committed supporter of everything I tried to do.

One such occasion was when Jo rang Gordon at his estate in Holmby Hills, Los Angeles, and told him that the vet had suggested a human orthopaedic surgeon might be able to help our little striped dependent. Gordon rang me and I explained the details.

"Make it happen," he said. There was never any discussion about cost. "Just make it happen."

With Jo's backing, Gordon agreed to foot any bill, so it was not long before my knight in shining armour appeared. He examined Horace, studied the x-rays which had been taken at London Zoo and measured his legs. Horace was oblivious. His only pain came where the fur had worn away on the sides of his legs as he pulled himself along, but he knew no different. The surgeon returned to his workshop and, soon afterwards, he delivered the special set of tiger splints, akin to the sort that a child suffering from a club foot might use. I fitted the leg irons and felt a wave of emotion as Horace stood for the first time, a look of happy confusion spreading across his face.

The doctor taught me various massage techniques that he felt would help and, sure enough, Horace soon progressed from an ungainly waddle to a clumsy walk. Every day would commence with our physiotherapy sessions and lots of words of encouragement. He would clank around in his irons and eventually progressed to running. I regarded it as a miracle when the splints were discarded. He would be barrel-chested for the rest of his life, but Horace suffered no ill effects from his shaky start to life. It made me realise the truth of the old adage: "where there's a will, there's a way".

Life was perfect but for one thing. My co-worker was sinking to new levels of inertia. I had no problem with doing the majority of the work, as I always felt that if you want a good job doing then you should do it yourself, but I was not prepared to compromise the well-being of the animals. By the time he turned up for work, I had got all the apes out of their bedrooms, given them breakfast and cleaned out their enclosures. That was one thing. However, I called in on a day off once to find all my chaps still in bed even though it was 11 in the morning. I rolled up my sleeves and got stuck into my normal routine. When my co-worker finally arrived, he was bemused by my concern.

I did not want to rock the boat so soon into a job I

loved, but felt I could not let it carry on, and so, with my heart in my mouth, I went to see Jo.

"Don't worry, Jeremy," she said. "Gordon's well aware of what he's like. The trouble is he's always told Gordon that there's no one else who would take over the role."

"You're joking," I gushed. "This is a dream job for most keepers."

Jo smiled. "Let's give it six months," she said. "If the situation has not improved by then, we'll make a change and you can run the place."

My satisfaction was tempered by my impatience at having to toil alongside someone with such a different approach from me for another six months. Needless to say, nothing did change and he was sent packing. Thereafter, I worked in splendid isolation for the rest of my years at Little Rhondda.

When I was free to take control of the collection, I worked hard and fast to raise standards of cleanliness, safety, diet and, in my opinion, general husbandry. I introduced various novel ways of encouraging the apes and cats to forage and hunt for their snacks, rather than merely tipping a heap of food on the feeding shelf. I also got busy with my welding torch and made many new toys and places for the chaps to hide, including water spray features to cool them down in the summer months. The current generation of animal care staff like to believe they invented things such as "operant conditioning" and "environmental enrichment", but the truth is some of us were using the same beneficial tricks years ago, only we didn't give the practice a fancy title.

When Jo and the kids moved to Los Angeles to be with Gordon, it was decided that I should move up to a flat in the main house. This was really hard to believe. A rags-to-pseudo-riches story. From begging in the streets, I was now living with my wife and son in a house valued at £6million. Not only that, but I was living with orangs and gorillas and tigers, with only the daily visits of the housekeeper to wake me from my dream world.

My primary interest remained in the anthropoid apes, but the pleasure I gleaned from my relationship with Horace was truly exceptional. At least once a day, I would take him for a walk around the pristine gardens of Little Rhondda, bedecked with colourful clusters of chrysanthemums. Inevitably, our route would be chosen by him. I fastened the heavy metal chain to his collar and we set off, him doing what he wanted and me striving to hold on. At any time he could have made a break for it and started worrying the stars down the road, because I doubt that the garden fence was tiger-proof, but Horace had all he wanted within the grounds. He would sniff around the greenhouses, under the nervous gaze of Arthur the gardener, and then cross the bottom lawns to check out the enclosure where his parents, Shere Khan and Rhanee, lived. Some days they would indulge in the tiger equivalent of a purr, but mostly they ignored their spoilt offspring. There was never a chance of reintroducing Horace to his mother after hand-rearing him. It just was not an option.

Next came Horace's favourite part of our morning constitutional, namely a dip in the Olympic-sized swimming pool. His pace would increase until he crashed into the water, dragging me along in his wake. Tigers love water and Horace would swim through the pool, almost drowning me as I clung to the 100-kilo pussycat, and then emerge to shake what seemed like 10 gallons of water from his fur at the other end. The saving grace for me was that the pool was covered in the winter, so I could dry out until spring, when the fun would begin again.

It was some months before I finally got to meet Gordon Mills. He was a dapper figure, who looked every inch the rock star himself, with the bouffant hair of the 1970s, tanned skin and trappings of fame. I was walking through the garden with Horace one day when he accosted me.

"Hey, what's he like in the car?" he said.

I had often taken Horace out in the back of my Transit van. Indeed, I had enjoyed the looks of bemusement, mingled with fear, on the faces of passersby when they heard an almighty roar from within the parked van as I did some shopping.

"He's fine in the van," I replied.

"Great," Gordon gushed. "Come on, then. Let's take him to see Ray."

"Er, are you sure?"

Gordon fixed me one of his looks. "What's the problem?"

"No problem," I quickly answered, knowing full well that Gordon had dismissed a previous employer for having the temerity to stand up to him.

Ray was Gilbert O'Sullivan's real name. He now lived in a mansion of his own in St George's Hill, not as big as Gordon's rock pile but still a lavish estate that befitted his status as a bona fide star earning millions every year. I was slightly nervous about keeping Horace under control and also about having my boss sit in my beaten-up old Transit van. That nervousness turned to downright fear when Gordon reappeared in his brand new, gleaming Mercedes.

"Come on," he shouted. "Get in."

The journey to Ray's was happily uneventful. Gordon parked up and bounded up the pathway, rapping on the door. Ray answered it and got the surprise of his life as Gordon breezed in, followed swiftly by an excitable tiger and a sweating keeper.

"Er, do you want a cup of tea?" Ray asked as Horace tore off upstairs to explore his new surroundings, me flailing behind him like a boy struggling with a kite in a gale.

Thankfully, we did not stay long. I think Gordon only wanted to go to see Ray's reaction. We said goodbye and headed towards the car. Unfortunately, Horace had decided he was having such a good time that he wanted to stay a little longer. I tried to shove him in the car but he would not budge. Then I went around the other side and tried pulling him. As Ray watched this bizarre scene, I could not help but think there was a good song in this somewhere.

Finally, Horace succumbed and Gordon hit the accelerator. Horace was now a disgruntled cat and he began frantically clawing at the seats. He did not use his mouth, as tigers only use that for killing and eating, but he was like a shredding machine and the back of the car was filled with foam and leather confetti. I knew that he was actually trying to dig the door out.

I breathed a sigh of relief when we arrived home and Horace jumped out. Back on familiar ground, he sat down in the sun as if nothing had happened. I got out and surveyed the damage. The plush leather seats had been ripped to pieces and there were holes in the floor. I was sure this would lead to my dismissal as I knew how much Gordon loved cars. I quickly dragged Horace away to his enclosure, cursing him under my breath, and then returned to face the music and the remains of the once magnificent car. I was surprised to find Gordon holding court in front of Jo and some employees, laughing at the damage wrought by his tiger. "It takes all sorts," I said to myself and slunk off into the darkest undergrowth I could find.

I survived and it was a happy time for me. I took Gordon and Jo's children to school, including the Clair immortalised in the Gilbert O'Sullivan song of the same name, and gained a bit of extra pocket money. When I moved to the flat in the main house, I commandeered the scullery for Horace's quarters, cleaned out the washing and reminded the other employees not to leave any doors open.

I respected Gordon and there is no doubt he loved his zoo. However, it was sometimes a balancing act between speaking my mind and being mindful of my position. That was certainly the case one night when the Millses returned and hosted one of their celebrity parties. I was in bed asleep when the phone went.

"Come on, I need you," Gordon said. I could tell he had been drinking. "We need to get to the ape house."

I didn't dare ask why at that point, but grabbed some clothes and hastily made my way down to the party. There were a group of people huddled around Gordon, including a very famous boxer.

"Ah, Jeremy. Look, my friend here thinks he could beat a gorilla in a fight. Well, there's only one way to find out."

I could scarcely believe what I was hearing. Clearly, they had been talking about the comparative strength of man and beast and, with a champion boxer at hand, had come up with this ridiculous suicide mission. So my task was to take the boxer down to see Ollie, our silverback bought from a Birmingham pet shop, so the debate could be settled once and for all.

I could not let this happen, but knew better than to

contradict Gordon in front of his celebrity pals. And so I began my slow traipse to the ape house, wondering how on earth I could get out of this fix. The drink meant nobody realised I was leading the mob along the most long-winded route possible, doubling back and meandering through the grounds like an alcohol-fuelled snake. I was striving to come up with an excuse, and so I decided to appeal to Gordon's sense of fair play.

"Look, this isn't right," I said to him. "Ollie's been in bed asleep so it's not fair to wake him up in the middle of the night."

Gordon seemed swayed by this argument, but we carried on in silence. The ape house was now in sight and I could not make any more deviations without rousing suspicion. "Why me?" I thought as the party of vigilantes grew increasingly excited in my wake. And it was just at that moment that the boxer threw up and fell down drunk in the bushes by the entrance. The fight was off.

5

Harry and Amy

THE NEXT DAY I threw caution to the wind and went into Gordon's personal office and removed every key that would give him access to the animals. It was a big risk on my part, but the thought of what might have happened had the pugilist not passed out in the bushes meant it was worth it. I later confessed what I had done but assured Gordon that I would accompany him to see his animals whenever he wished. I always found him fair in such matters. It was knowing how to handle him, as had been the case when he barged straight into my flat without a knock or a shout.

"What on earth do you think you're doing?" I said.

Not used to being spoken to like that, he replied, "It's my house, you know."

"It's your house but it's my home. Next time you knock."

It was a case of picking your fights and knowing when to stand up to him, but certainly you didn't undermine him in front of his friends.

I was in my element, though, running what was such an extraordinary private collection. I continued to make lots of improvements, especially when it came to giving the chaps something to do in their homes and in terms of cleanliness; I have always been very fastidious about that.

The morals of that time might be questionable now, but they were accepted then. The way they used to acquire animals makes me shudder today, but everyone did it. David Attenborough was off on his zoo quests, taking animals from the wild as part of his collecting expeditions for London Zoo and the BBC, as was Gerald Durrell, who has done as much for conservation as anyone. Money changed hands and dealers were used, often regardless of their legitimacy. I knew that Gordon had got our gorillas from a bona fide Dutch dealer, but these animals would have been brutally seized from the wild, which would have probably meant the mother being shot and the babies wrenched away. It was a dreadful trade and numerous babies perished, but at the time I was concerned with keeping the survivors alive. I had no idea that one day I would be taking on the poachers and smugglers.

I knew that some infant gorillas had perished at Little Rhondda before I arrived. So Gordon visited the Dutch dealer looking for more mature replacements. He was shown two males. While the trader dealt with another matter, Gordon noted the two animals "mating" and so he surmised that the dealer had wrongly sexed the gorillas, and that this was actually a valuable breeding pair. The deal was struck and Memba and Margo were shipped to England before the Dutchman realised his mistake. For several months, Gordon's favoured after-dinner story concerned the time he had pulled the wool over the Dutchman's eyes.

This was all unbeknown to me until I noticed Margo urinating one day and producing an impressive fountain in an arc. I had a closer look. "What's this?" I asked myself. "Looks suspiciously like a willy to me." And that was how Margo became Monty.

When I informed Gordon he was incredulous. I had to tell him how gorilla males are the worst endowed of all primates and how, pre-maturity, there are no dimorphic differences between them and the females. Gordon had boasted of the "mating" episode in Holland to his friends and now had to alter his after-dinner story so that it became the case of the gay gorillas.

Buying and selling were part of life in those days and we were at the whim of fashion. During Gordon's long absences, I kept him updated with regular telephone bulletins, my main concern always being to keep his enthusiasm alive. Breeding was a real badge of honour and, despite his good humour, the disappointment when Margo became Monty hurt. Katie, meanwhile, was only three and we would have to wait another five years before she reached her sexual maturity. Then Belle Vue Zoo in Manchester closed down in 1977, and I had the perfect window of opportunity to indulge Gordon's desire for some new animals and my preferences for orang-utans.

Being flavour of the month, the Belle Vue gorillas were quickly snapped up, but I focused on their orangs. I developed a friendly relationship with the zoo's director, Peter Grayson, and secured their quartet for our collection at Little Rhondda at a cost of £15,000. I must confess to pangs of guilt when recalling this, but it was a perfectly acceptable transaction at the time. Back then, the buying and selling of endangered species were commonplace, unlike today, when no money ever changes hands when animals are moved between zoological establishments.

One day when I was on the phone to Peter to arrange the transportation of the four orangs, I heard a staff member burst into his office in the background.

"Bobo's given birth!" she cried.

Peter spoke calmly into the receiver. "Better make that five."

The extra apes meant I had to find some room. I did this by rehoming two old lady gorillas, Tessy and Flossy, along with Monty. I had been approached by an agent for Longleat Safari Park, who was clearly anxious to secure gorillas to live on an island in Half Mile Lake in the shadow of the Marquis of Bath's stately home. Shamefully, I accepted £15,000 for Gordon's purse to offload the gorillas. My guilt was exacerbated many years later when Monty fell into the Longleat lake and drowned.

Primate conservation had really taken off by then. Diane Fossey was well established as the gorilla guru and Jane Goodall was becoming similarly renowned for her behavioural work with chimpanzees. Along with Birute Galdikas, the three became known as Leakey's angels, in reference to their sponsor Louis

Leakey. Inevitably, it was Galdikas's work that most attracted me, as she had gone to Borneo at the start of the 1970s in search of the elusive red ape.

There were many debates and meetings to discuss gorilla conservation. Because Gordon's collection was very valuable, in terms of knowledge as well as money, I was invited to attend the Anthropoid Ape Advisory Panel. I never fitted in at these meetings. Zoo directors would offer idealistic advice and utopian thoughts about what should be done with the various apes in Britain. Everybody frowned upon the suitability of Longleat as a home for our gorillas, but nobody offered a solution.

I knew I was an outsider when I rushed to one such meeting at Twycross Zoo. I had no time to change after cleaning out the animals and so, covered in mud and worse, I jumped into Gordon's Rolls-Royce Corniche and drove the 150 miles to the Midlands. I was late and so I covered the distance in record time, pulling to a halt in a hail of stones next to a lowly Ford. I will never forget the look of disdain on the Bristol Zoo director's face as he got out of that car and watched this foul, unkempt apparition tumble from a gold Roller in decaying wellies. Like the rest, he was dressed in his finest suit, whereas I looked like a hippie at best.

I did not fit into the panel's rigid categories as I was both zoo director and janitor and every role in between. There was also some jealousy because I had more control over a very important collection than they did over their zoos. They would speak their idealistic garbage with no thought to the reality of how we would look after these apes. Many had merely inherited their positions from their fathers, and the snobbery and social climbing of zoo politics would never cease to leave me baffled and bemused.

I had other things to worry about at that Twycross meeting, though, because this was my first time back there since my midnight flit from the freezing caravan. Molly Badham and Nat Evans were there and it was an awkward reunion. By the time of the second panel meeting, we began speaking again, although nobody ever mentioned what had happened. It was as if it had been airbrushed from history and I was grateful for Molly's forgiving nature.

With the gorillas gone, I arranged the crates, lorry and driver to transport the five orange people some 230 miles south from Manchester to Surrey. Bobo rode with her new daughter, Kumang, as I had named her, and all five were warm and comfortable in their bedding crates. Kumang suckled her mother several times on the long journey, but I was hugely relieved when we finally got the newcomers into their homes and lush beds of wood wool. It was long after midnight when I turned the lights out, but to save money I returned the rented van to the hire company that same night.

One of the five came with a reputation. He was a very impressive male who was in his prime, with magnificent face flanges and a long wedding veil of a hairdo. He was known by all in Manchester as Harry the Bastard because he had bitten the toes off one of his previous carers in a rather unfortunate accident. This was only one of numerous disagreements they had had with him, but I marvelled at his appearance and formed a very good relationship with him. To me, Harry the Bastard was a very fair and amicable fellow.

Gordon indulged me from afar and allowed me to keep various of my own animals around the property. Over the years I added capuchin monkeys, crab-eating macaques, raccoons and reptiles. We had alligators, tortoises, terrapins and an Indian rock python that grew from 18 inches to 18 feet, weighed 12 stone and ended up living with me.

I also developed a fascination with birds and established several breeding pairs of road-damaged owls. I became fairly successful at artificially incubating and rearing them. I even had a go at a primitive form of falconry, giving injured kestrels, buzzards and sparrowhawks the opportunity of flight prior to release. Gordon himself went 50-50 with me on a pair of snowy owls from Jersey and Edinburgh zoos.

It was through the owls that I developed a friendship with Robin and Mary Haigh, who operated a wild animal sanctuary in nearby Chertsey. I went to them looking for food for my growing population of owls and ended up using my welding skills to make a string of barbecues and trailers, which Robin sold. Through Robin I also came across a talented jeweller and sculptor named Paul Eaton, who would turn his hand to anything to fund his art. All were friends who would be invaluable to me during the birth of Monkey World.

Fashion changes, apparently, and by the end of the 1970s tigers were becoming very last year. Everybody had them and they were breeding with regularity. This was before birth control had been introduced in zoos and tigers were now almost impossible to relocate, so I had a sense of trepidation when Gordon, no doubt influenced by his accountant, Bill Smith, said we had to let them go. They were Gordon's least favourite part of the collection and I could sympathise, because the anthropoid apes, and especially the orangs, gave me most pleasure. But it was going to be a big challenge.

Knowing how fond I was of Horace, Gordon offered him to me as a gift. I was thrilled, although I quickly did my sums and realised it would cost me half my salary to keep a full-grown tiger. One night I went to the circus and started chatting with the lion tamer, Martin Lacy, who had run a long-defunct zoo in Hucknall. He told me how cheap it was to feed his lions with the unsellable cuts from abattoirs. It was a lifeline and I soon struck a deal with a company in nearby Dorking. My relief at being able to keep Horace on my modest wages was huge.

I still had five tigers to rehome. I phoned every zoo I could think of and Colchester agreed to take our pair of Siberian cats. I called upon the services of Paul Eaton to help move them. We started work in the wee small hours and managed to crate the tigers and, with a cunningly devised winch, hauled the two boxes into the back of the van. The apes, meanwhile, were universally disgusted at me for rousing them so early, but I needed to clean their cages and provide them with enough food to last until my return before we set off. Finally, we hit the road and I dreaded to think what might happen if we were involved in an accident, but other than causing a few looks of horror as roars emerged from our van, the trip was routine.

Sadly, the tigers did not settle and we soon made the trip back to Colchester Zoo to pick them up. Finally, Longleat agreed to take all five, with the proviso that this was a donation and that I would also leave my crates with them. It was to be another early start. I had borrowed a lorry and the crates were tied to the sliding doors of the tigers' cage. All they had to do the next morning was walk out, tempted by the meat I'd leave for them in the crates, and the doors would slide shut on them, leaving them ready to be wheeled towards the lorry. I had also fastened ramps to the rear of the lorry and the winch was in place. Everything was ready for the Monday morning departure. And then, late on the Sunday night, I got a call from Paul's family. He had mangled his jaw in an accident with a garage door and was in hospital. Apparently, even in his semi-conscious state, he was mumbling about how bad he felt for letting me down.

"Not as bad as I'm going to make him feel when I see him" was my unsympathetic reply.

It made for an even earlier start and even unhappier apes. I had ensured the tigers were all hungry and so, tempted by a piece of meat, they crated with ease. I counted my blessings that these crates, borrowed from Robin Dunham, the assistant manager of Chessington World of Adventures, were on wheels. I would not have been able to cope otherwise. I made the trip to Longleat and returned to put the apes to bed. Then I dashed down the A3 to Guildford to visit Paul on his sickbed, where he was so apologetic that I felt quite guilty about my remark the previous night.

Working from home meant that I got to spend more time with my son than most fathers manage. I would wheel my way over to the orang-utans and leave Jamie in the pram while I carried out my work. Some of the more maternal apes clearly enjoyed his presence and would alert me if he became distressed. But Jamie was generally a contented, happy child, whose only requirements were constant hugs and a regular supply of wholesome food. That is not unlike a baby orang and, luckily, one of Jamie's favourite dishes was Mazuri primate diet. The first time Jamie caused me any trouble was when he was three and he decorated Jo Mills's new Mercedes sports car with an aerosol can. My heart sank again and I feared the sack. It was a repeat of Horace and our ill-fated trip to see Gilbert O'Sullivan. Luckily, Jo found the vandalism as amusing as Gordon had that time.

If you live among animals then you know that when death comes, it must be treated as a part of life. I had discovered the cruelty of this when I was still a small boy and my pet monkey, Fred, had died. That left me devastated and I retreated into myself. Father gave a dramatic speech that night, imbued with all the gravitas and thespian skill he could muster.

"There is livestock and there is deadstock," he said as if treading the boards at the Royal Shakespeare Company. "You have to get used to it. Life goes on. It is a never-ending circle. When a animal dies the best thing to do is and go and spend time with the ones that are still living." Father really should have been on the stage, but his words did resonate. However, the day you get used to an animal dying is the day you should get out of this world and move on.

When Bobo the orang-utan died after a short illness, it left Kumang motherless at the tender age of 18 months. Although semi-weaned, Kumang still needed constant maternal care. I tried to do my best, but it was not easy. The conundrum is: how do you feed an orang that's as strong as a horse and as obstinate as a donkey? Kumang would spit out her milk and was very wary of me, having previously seen me only from the sanctuary of her mother's arms. That was why she developed a rather spiteful streak and clamped her teeth down on my hand one day. The pain was excruciating and I lost two fingernails in the blood, but I patched myself up and went back to my task. After three days of spending every available moment with her and sleeping at her side, Kumang relented and snuggled into me. She was soon in a very deep sleep as she held herself tightly in my arms.

Our relationship developed from that moment and I dismissed the missing fingernails as part of the learning curve. The situation is the same when it comes to children – they can cause you a lot of grief, but it is worth it in the end. Kumang would spend her days in what had been the gorilla house and come back and spend the night in my flat. The aim was to reintroduce her to the other orangs, so Kumang would accompany Jamie and me as we went about our normal care routines, having daily contact with her kinfolk through the wire mesh. One of them was Louis. At the time I kept orangs and gorillas together and, while that would no doubt offend the Anthropoid Ape Advisory Panel, there was no reason why they could not co-exist. Louis was an adult orang and he was fine with the younger male gorillas. It was only when they got older and they started pushing Louis around, for sport not spite, that I moved him.

I always had a soft spot for Louis who, like me, seemed to suffer from terrible headaches and would hold his head in his hands. I still remembered my mother insisting my migraines were psychosomatic. "It still hurts," I would protest to no avail. I tried to be nicer to Louis.

Life, as I was already painfully aware, was a series of peaks and troughs. And so, as my relationship with Kumang improved, my marriage to Gill crumbled. It was amicable and there was no one else involved, but it would mean I only got to see Jamie every other weekend, which was a crushing blow.

It was sad that we could not make it work, and it has been pointed out to me subsequently that working with animals is not conducive to living with humans. But I don't think I have ever changed. I think there is an impression that what I do is very romantic, but the reality is very different. And I never said that I would stop working so hard when I got married. I do this seven days a week and my personal commitment is huge. My opinion on my relationship with Gill is that she knew what I was like when she came into my life, and if that wasn't a problem then, why should it be one now?

There were more changes afoot, too, as Jo Mills returned from the States to live in the house. That meant I went to live in the thatched gatehouse within the grounds. In this state of flux, I threw myself into work for distraction.

One day Katie the gorilla fell sick. She had eaten a bundle of straw and it had compacted in her stomach. She was really very poorly and I gave her a series of micro enemas in the hope it would bring her back, but she was weak and wouldn't rally. I took to sleeping with her in the gorilla house for a week. Jo produced a millionaire's banquet for us, full of anchovies, fine cheese and handmade biscuits, which she had bought from a local deli. I looked at the feast and marvelled at some of the exotic foods on display. Katie was ambivalent and not hungry, but I hadn't eaten for days, so I turned my back and started nibbling away. "Oh, that's good," I said to myself. Consumed by the array of goods in front of me, I was slow to sense Katie standing at my shoulder. She reached out for a biscuit, but I flicked her hand away.

"Get lost, you," I said. "You had your chance."

Nevertheless, I was relieved to see Katie back on her feet. A couple more nights and it was clear that she was going to live. The enemas had worked and her appetite for life was returning. I decided it was time to put her back in with some of the others and deemed that Coco the orang would be the one likely to give her the least grief.

It was late when I returned to the ape house. I went in and was giving Katie her medicine when, from out of nowhere, Coco darted over. He wanted the medicine too. "Bugger off, Coco," I cried. "You've had your treat."

My words fell on deaf ears and I soon found myself pinned to the ground by a male orang, while Katie looked on. I pushed Coco's head away, but he managed to administer one superficial bite. We were rolling around on the floor, somewhere in the middle of a millionaire's isolated estate, for what seemed like hours. Finally, I managed to lever him off and make it out of the cage.

"Jesus!" I thought. "What on earth got into him?"

I took a few steps and realised my slippers had come off in the melee. That was when my brain took leave of my head and I decided to go back in to fetch them. Whereupon the whole thing happened again.

It was my own fault. You have to respect wild animals and expect the unexpected. The incident did nothing to dampen my enthusiasm for the orange people. That enthusiasm was fired further when I noted the tell-tale swelling near Jane's bottom. I knew these grape-sized growths on orangs were more accurate than any pregnancy test. Jane had arrived from Manchester with a poor record of motherhood, but Gordon and I were very excited and hoped she might have turned over a new leaf.

It was wishful thinking. When Rimba arrived, Jane showed no interest in caring for her daughter at all. I had no option but to take the newcomer away as she was going to starve to death very quickly if I didn't. I called the vet, who arrived and anaesthetised Jane so that we could remove Rimba. And so began a three-month ordeal of trying to keep her alive. With no natural instinct to feed, it became a force-feeding exercise, with me striving desperately to get some milk into her mouth, while she just lay in my lap in total indifference. I would try this every two hours and would set my alarm clock so I never missed a feed. It was gruelling and frustrating and, sure enough, in the early hours of one morning, Rimba passed away. I couldn't help wondering whether Jane knew something that I didn't when she had shown no inclinations towards being a mother to her baby.

Two years later, Jane fell pregnant again and the cycle

repeated itself. Jane refused to feed Jambi and so once again I had to remove the baby and attempt to hand-rear her. Jambi was even more fragile than Rimba had been, weighing only one kilogram and refusing to suck on any nipple. Unable to maintain her body temperature, she was also at constant risk of hypothermia, so I put her in a human incubator I had hired and dressed her in babygros. The final, depressing similarity with Rimba was that Jambi also gave up and died at the three-month hurdle, which had now become an invisible brick wall.

The Anthropoid Ape Advisory Panel did not help my gloomy mood when they said that Coco, our single Sumatran orang, should be living with others of his sub-species, rather than with the Borneo orange people we had. I realised the value of trying to perpetuate the species, but also had the nagging suspicion that this was another example of idealism riding over practicality. Nevertheless, it was decided. Coco would go to Bristol Zoo and we would get James from Borneo in return. John Crittal, a very good local vet who was in charge of Wimbledon dog track, came down and darted Coco with the anaesthetic, ketamine. He added a sedative to avoid the hallucinogenic side effects that made this a designer drug.

We had a surprise when we arrived at Bristol. Mike Colbourne, the senior ape keeper, greeted me and Paul with the words: "Hello, I'm Mike and I'm a homosexual."

"I'm Jeremy and your secret's safe with me," I replied.

Mike later came to work at Monkey World, where he remains a valued member of staff, and we have discussed that episode. Although he is gay, he cannot remember quite why he said that but suspects it had been a bet.

The rest of the Bristol staff arrived, all dressed in matching surgical gowns, which Paul found most amusing. By contrast with Coco, James proved difficult to crate. Several darts from the Bristol vet had failed before one had an impact. However, he was underdosed, so they had to top him up with several more drugs. We endured a nervous trip back, as he slept for the entire journey and we wondered whether we would be able to wake him up again. Luckily, we were.

James, through no fault of his own, failed to settle at Little Rhondda. Coco, too, was unhappy in Bristol and was therefore moved to Dudley Zoo. Eventually, I brought Coco home and took James to Dudley. I was left wondering about the practical knowledge of the

Anthropoid Ape Advisory Panel.

Things got worse still in 1981, when Harry the so-called Bastard died. One of the problems with anthropoid apes is that they don't show symptoms of illness. To do so in the wild would leave them vulnerable. Recently, it has been shown that apes actually practise homeopathy and, when ill, eat certain plants, but the research is still in its infancy. In captivity, it is easy to miss symptoms at the very point when you want to nip something in the bud. Only in his last couple of days was it clear that Harry was unwell. In fact, he had abscesses on his liver. I called the vet. He gave him antibiotics. If an animal is well enough you will anaesthetise it so you can take blood samples and examine it. Harry, though, was too far gone and died on Boxing Day. To compound my misery, my back gave up as I tried to move his 80-kilogram body. And so I was left lying on the floor beside my dead pal, crippled in agony, doused by relentless rain.

There was little time for wallowing in self-pity. I remembered what my father had said about coping by concentrating on the animals that are still alive. It was a never-ending circle. Rosie, one of our Manchester ladies, gave birth, but sadly the baby was stillborn. Daisy, another of the orangs, gave birth to Pongo, who suffered from polycystic fibrous dysplasia, which is pretty much what the Elephant Man had. The bone wasn't calcified and was more like cartilage that had grown out of control, to the extent that it restricted his ability to eat, drink or even breathe. The poor chap was one in a million. How unlucky could you get. He lasted six months before he died.

Jane was also pregnant again by Louis and the cycle continued. It was a low ebb in my life. It had become clear that Gordon was thinking about closing his zoo and my personal life was in disarray. Being parted from Jamie was hard to take and the memory of Harry's death was still vivid. It was into this state of flux and depression that a frail hairball named Amy was first introduced on September 23, 1983. Nothing would be quite the same again.

6

The Living Dead

AMY WEIGHED JUST two pounds and two ounces. She was a slip of a thing. Like both Rimba and Jambi before her, she could not maintain her own body temperature, and she seemed to lack the necessary will to live. She was born into a fight for survival and her prospects were a dark shade of grey.

I went about my time-honoured and hitherto unsuccessful routine. Within three hours of her birth, I had Amy in the incubator. The vet had already got it for me from the local hospital. I had estimated her arrival date accurately. An orang-utan pregnancy is very like a human one. It lasts approximately 250 days and ends with contractions and the waters breaking. The main difference is that the birth is usually much easier and less painful. In a nutshell, the orang is not such a wuss! Meanwhile, the human diet has developed to such a high-protein composition that our babies are massive by comparison. Result – it hurts.

Amy's arrival was trouble-free, but from the moment she appeared she was in grave peril. I clothed her in baby-gros and gave her two-hourly feeds. Like her sisters, she was utterly uninterested in feeding. All she wanted to do was cling onto me, which is the natural reaction of a helpless, defenceless baby orang. I had become her mother and she gripped onto me around my middle and dug in for dear life.

I didn't let her out of the house. I knew that any infection or cold could have killed her. Amy stayed indoors and I wore a mask. I was desperate not to limit her modest chances and I avoided contact with anyone who was ill or even knew anybody who was ill. That was not too much of a difficulty for me as I preferred to live a happy solitary existence with the animals on the estate.

I was mentally, physically and emotionally exhausted. The sleep deprivation left me feeling permanently jet-lagged and I did not think I could take another failure. My mind was muddled and the only thing that gave it some clarity was the bundle of misery in the incubator. In those early days, it was a juggling act. I felt like I was her protector and only chance, but I also knew that at some point I needed to expose her to build up some immunity. It is the same as with your kids, but multiplied by 10 because orangs are so delicate and vulnerable.

She stayed in the incubator for two months, which is a lot longer than she should have done, but she was so groggy that there was no choice. One day, I realised I would have to turn off the lamps and hope the constant feeds had built up some semblance of strength.

It remained hard work. I made a new home for her by fixing a plywood box with a Perspex front onto a TV stand so I could wheel her around. I christened this contraption Evil Edna and introduced it to Amy. Orangs are designed to live in the treetops, not on the floor. They are not made for walking around on the ground and really have four hands for clinging onto things; if you live in a tree then it's best not to let go as it's a long way down. So when you have an orang at home you need to satisfy that dependency. They need to hang onto something. I started with a teddy and put one in Edna and drifted off to sleep, craving a few minutes' rest before I was woken for the next feed. Fat chance. My eyes opened as if spring-loaded to a cacophony of sound. Amy was in utter hysterics. I threw off the covers and rushed to the side of Edna where Amy was screaming. I realised she had rolled on top of the teddy and was panicking because she had nothing to grab onto.

I ran to the bathroom and grabbed a towel and rolled it up. I took this back into the bedroom and put it next to Amy. When she had stopped doing her best Violet Elizabeth and "scweaming until she was thick", she grabbed onto the towel with her feet as if it were a perch. The comfort was instant. Amy settled down and looked at me with her brown saucer eyes. It was as if she was saying, "Don't ever do that again, okay?"

I counted down the days, and when she was three months old, I felt a surge of pride and panic. This had been the insurmountable barrier for Rimba and Jambi, so I felt it was both a cornerstone and a milepost.

"So you think life is worth living after all?" I asked her that night. She was hanging on, both to the towel and to life.

She continued to live in Evil Edna in those first few months. I would feed her, she would grip her towel and then, in the evening, I would wheel her into the lounge and we would watch television together. It was touch and go because she still would not feed. It was not anorexia but she would just refuse to take milk. The whole experience was exceptional in all my dealings with hand-rearing. I tried to give her longer between feeds, hoping that would make her hungry, but it didn't make any difference. She could go two, four and six hours. It meant I had to force-feed her, which is horrible, but it was for the greater good. The trouble is the more you fight an orang the more you lose. Slowly, though, with each passing day, and with each ounce of milk drunk, I felt more confident.

I still had our other orangs and gorillas to care for, not to mention all the other animals, and it was becoming a problem giving Amy the constant care she needed. That was how Meryl McCaully came into my life. She was a local woman and I employed her to help rear Amy in those first precious months while I ensured the other animals got the attention they needed. Meryl's mother, Ann, was a trained midwife, so she also helped out and before long Amy was growing.

The wider world looked bleak, though. I knew the end was nigh when I picked up the morning post and found forms for export licences. I rang Gordon.

"What are all these licence forms?" I asked.

"Oh nothing," he replied. "Just in case."

I was not a fool and knew what was coming. It was not long before Gordon told me the inevitable.

"I'm sorry, Jeremy, but you know, times are hard."

"Come on, Gordon, cut to the chase."

"Well, I'm giving up. We're going to have to get rid of the animals."

It was not a shock and in some ways it was a relief that the uncertainty was over, but it was still a body blow. I was going to have to move out and there was no way I would be able to keep a tiger with me. I walked down to the tiger enclosure, empty but for the familiar face of my barrel-chested chum, Horace, and listened to the ghosts of Shere Khan and the others. I was sad for myself but scared for Horace. I knew the problems I had encountered trying to rehome the other tigers. Where once they had been coveted, they were now deemed surplus to requirements. Everyone seemed to have tigers and the females would have a litter of three or four cubs every year. You could not give them away.

I left Horace and went back to the gatehouse. I checked on Amy, who was contentedly sitting in Evil Edna, and then I picked up the phone. I had a long list of numbers but felt, deep down, that what I was doing was an empty gesture. Sure enough, no zoo I rang showed any interest in taking another tiger.

"I'm sorry, we've got plenty," said one director.

Another laughed. "You've got no chance."

I worked my way through every zoo in Britain and got the same response. I even started to ring some zoos abroad. Even with the language problem, it was easy to understand the bad news. I made more than 100 mercy calls but nobody could help.

I knew what the answer was before I got it but I had to try. For Horace. We had been through so much and his sorry start in life mirrored Amy's. But now, as Amy began to feed and thrive, Horace's time was up. Every door was shut and I faced the horrible reality.

After spending days making calls to zoos, even offering to throw in a splendid travelling crate and all the food I had, I had to make another call to David Taylor, who had become our vet.

I shook his hand when he arrived and together we walked down to Horace's enclosure. I could have chosen to lock myself away but I was in this until the bitter end. I felt I owed Horace that much. David loaded the dart and took aim. The sound of the dart thudding into Horace was agony. When he was asleep,

David gave him an intravenous dose of barbiturates. I cannot even begin to communicate how this affected me. I was in a bad place at the time and this was the ultimate kick in the teeth. I confess that I didn't cry when either of my parents died, but I did with Horace.

I had just been made redundant and my marriage was over. I felt like I had lost my son because he was living with his mother and now Horace was gone too. The tiger enclosures roared their silence and I felt totally deflated. There are few sadder places than vacant animal enclosures, a vivid reminder of what you have lost and a guarantee to leave you feeling just as empty inside.

I have always tried to be practical in such circumstances. I do everything I possibly can for animals when they are alive and I have my memories, but I have no emotion for a dead body and I don't need any trophies. Everyone has their own morals and, perhaps it sounds callous to some, but I sold Horace to a taxidermist for £150. That was a huge sum of money in those days and I knew it would help with caring for Amy and the rest. Call it the circle of life or whatever you will.

It was nevertheless a horrible thought that dear old Horace was worth more dead than alive.

7

Apes on a Plane

It was two years earlier, on July 28, 1981, when I first met Jim Cronin. On a rare afternoon off from working at Little Rhondda, I borrowed Gordon's car and took his daughters, Beverley and Tracy Mills, down to Howletts Zoo with me. John Aspinall, the owner, was a Mills family friend and was happy for the girls to wander around while I toured the enclosures.

I ended up in the café, a wooden shed in the middle of the park, waiting for Beverley and Tracy to return. It was there that I came across a brash New Yorker with an unkempt hairdo and equally wild enthusiasm. He stood out, partly because of his accent and mannerisms, but also because he was the only one of the zoo staff, sitting around drinking coffee, who showed any interest in what I was doing at Little Rhondda.

"Do you think I could come and have a look?" he asked.

"Yes, sure," I said. I was instantly attracted to his energy and it was not long before I was sucked into his infectious pipe dream.

"What I want is a cageless park specialising in rescued primates," he told me as we walked around the enclosures at Weybridge, then still full and vibrant. "Have you heard of Wim Mager?"

"Who?"

"He's Dutch. Used to be a photographer. His concept was to have a park where apes could wander around in huge, forest-like enclosures. I want to do something like that here."

"Okay."

"Nobody takes me seriously," he said.

"Why?"

"They think I'm a loudmouth Yank living in a fantasy world. I couldn't care less. I'm going to make this happen."

Jim's eyes went through his bushy eyebrows when he saw my facilities and, two weeks later, he turned up with a van full of steel. I got my welder out and created some makeshift cages which I put in the gorilla house kitchen. Jim was already in contact with several British laboratories by that point and needed places to keep the monkeys he was getting. So my cages quickly became homes to three pairs of red-bellied tamarins and five marmosets.

It is testament to Jim's eagerness not to take advantage of me that he helped with the welding. Helped, perhaps, is the wrong word. Later Jim would confide that he thought Manual Labour was a Spanish tradesman; his practical skills were practically non-existent. However, his real gift was an excessive amount of compassion, and he was brilliant when it came to the dietary, social, scientific and theoretical aspects of animal welfare. We got on so well because, other than animals, we had precisely nothing in common.

Over the next few months, we would speak every night and I would give blow-by-blow updates on his monkeys, especially when both the tamarins and marmosets became pregnant. This was a reflection on the diets that Jim had devised, comprising human baby cereal with added vitamins, and the carefully controlled heat, humidity and light that I provided. We fast became a team. When one of the marmosets gave birth, the baby, Timothy, was rejected by his mother and so took to living in my hair. Well, it was wild.

Meanwhile, Jim would tell me about any latest developments in his endless search for a site and money for his park. It looked a distant dream and I spent three years transporting him around in a beat-up VW as he counted the pennies and cost of his obsession. At the end of each conversation, I would always revert to my Derbyshire accent and say to Jim, "I'll sithee." For some reason, he found that very amusing.

When Gordon said he was closing his collection, Jim came to my aid and took the small ex-laboratory monkeys to Howletts with him. My friends, Robin and Mary, rehomed some of my raptors and I managed to keep Ermentrude the python. It was, however, a grim period in my life and I was grateful to have Amy to occupy my thoughts.

She was still very dependent and would cling around my shoulders like an Angora backpack as I walked around. Sometimes I even had to take her to the shops, which was always an event. Amy would sit in the passenger seat or, more often, hang upside down in the back window, gurning at other cars and enjoying the chaos she wrought. I hate to think how many crashes we may have caused on these excursions. In the shops or on the streets there were two main reactions that I found to be a very good illustration of human behaviour. Some people would come up and be interested. "Isn't she cute?" would be a common comment. The majority, however, had that very British attitude, the stiff upper lip and almost obsessive reserve. So they would think to themselves, "This is not an orang-utan I see before me." They would then edge away and pretend everything in the high street was quite normal.

Amy took a lot of looking after because she was a chip off the old block. Just like her mother, Jane, she was inherently bloody-minded. Her modus operandi was "because I can". It is always interesting to note how orangs have different personalities. When Jane's group came to us from Belle Vue, she quickly stood out as an independent lady, and Amy was the same. I would often speak to her and point out her shortcomings.

"Yes, yes, good for you, now can we get on with it, please?"

"I'm on your side."

"You've made your point."

"Can we both get a life, please?"

"Of all the orang-utans in all the world, why did I end up with you?"

Nevertheless, it was Amy who diverted me from

wallowing in negative thoughts about being jobless, homeless and broke.

A baby orang is conditioned to hang onto its mother. It takes a long time, certainly several months, before it detaches itself and starts to do things for itself. I made sure I laid down the ground rules very early on. If I was watching television and Amy was plucking things from the bookshelf then I would raise my voice.

"You've got your things and I've got mine," I told her as I scooped up the scattered pages. "Let's keep it that way." I may be a hippie but I am also a disciplinarian.

I was happy to have Amy around, though, because I believe orangs are like human babies and they need love and attention just as much. It always amazes me that parents have a baby and then put it in the farthest room in the house and rig up a baby-listening device. Did you want the baby? People wonder why little Tommy grew up to be a degenerate. They say, "We gave him everything." Well, they might have given him money and food, but did they give him a hug when he needed it? That's what matters and it applies to apes as well as humans.

It is not easy, of course. Hand-rearing Amy meant I couldn't do anything for myself that took longer than

20 minutes. I ended up being unable to see straight. I barely had more than an hour's unbroken sleep and, although I loved her, I looked forward to the day when I could throw her out of the house.

Amy and I were still literally attached to each other in 1984, but I knew I would have to leave her soon. Gordon had arranged to ship our five gorillas and seven orangs to San Diego Zoo. There was no fee involved. This was a donation but, given the value of the collection, Gordon did get a huge amount of tax relief as a result. Moving them was a monumental task, so I shelved my job-hunting to help co-ordinate it. Six days before we flew out to America, the San Diego team arrived. There were two vets, Don Jansen and Phil Robinson, and two primate care leaders, Gail Foland and Chuck Henderson. We hit it off immediately, especially when I declared my dislike of the American race.

"Ahh, Jeez," said Phil. "How we love your English sense of humour."

The San Diego team were consummate pros and had provided splendid shipping crates that filled me with confidence. No expense was spared. I had been used to this approach with Gordon, whose solution for any problem was to throw money at it. Jim would later adopt the same philosophy, the only difference being he didn't actually have any money.

I arranged for Amy to stay with Chris Anscombe, the ape manager at Chessington Zoo, and his experienced mother. The next morning, bright and early, the phone went.

"I can't look after this orang," Chris said. "She's too much like hard work."

Amy had exhibited her most obdurate streak during her one night at the Anscombes', refusing to be fed and no doubt sulking at being discarded by her surrogate mum.

"I can't cope," Chris said. "She's got too many peculiar ways."

I reverted to Plan B, which was to take Amy to Chertsey where my good friends, Robin and Mary, would look after her. They were already well versed in her whims and idiosyncrasies. I left Amy knowing she was in good hands and hoping there would not be another frantic phone call in the morning.

Amy had no idea that her parents were being shipped off. I had not tried to reintroduce her because I knew it was pointless. She was too dependent at that time so now Louis and Jane were emigrating. Jim arrived at 7am on the day of departure and I felt pleasantly smug at the number of apes we managed to inject with anaesthetics using an ordinary syringe, rather than the more stressful darting method. This is another development that modern wild animal care staff believe is their own.

By midnight the apes were all packed into their crates and stacked on two lorries. We then made the short trip to Heathrow Airport, where they were secured to pallets, ready for loading the following morning. Louis was intrigued by the day's events and found that by holding onto the mesh cover and kicking out with both feet, he could move his box. Thus, an orangutan explored a cavernous warehouse at Heathrow from the inside of a slowly shuffling cube.

The plan was to fly by 737 cargo plane to Frankfurt and then change to a 747, which would be half cargo and half passengers, for the long haul to California. Regulations decreed that only Phil and I could attend to the animals in Germany, but we could all be in contact with the chaps for the remainder of the trip. We were allocated the row of seats against the bulkhead which separated us from them, but we all agreed it would be much better to be in the hold with them. My travelling companions on that voyage included Meryl, whom I was now dating, and after some excited talk, we settled down with our own thoughts by the crates.

"I bet there's not many people who have flown over the North Pole in such company," I said as I looked around. After a long pause I thought I had better add, "I mean the apes."

When the crew landed the plane, the rest of us remained on automatic pilot. I climbed into a truck and made my way to the San Diego Wild Animal Park, rather than the zoo itself; another truck with some of the other animals was heading there. The chaps were quickly installed in their new bedrooms and, while they had a meal, we went off to our own hotel. You might have thought I would sleep for a month after the events of the past few days and the stress and traumas that preceded them, but I was up at dawn to take a photograph of the sunrise over a palm tree.

"What the hell are you doing?" shouted Meryl, but I was happy. I had wanted the picture and was not going to miss it. It was March 30, 1984 and I calculated it was my first break from work for 2,845 days. I was happy to look through the viewfinder and forget the bigger picture.

We spent the next six weeks helping the San Diego zoo staff to settle the chaps into their new lives. It was not hard, given the exceptional facilities, the dedicated staff and the sub-tropical climate. Our hosts were wonderful, too, and took us everywhere from Mexico to Disneyland. If I had to say goodbye to these great apes, I could think of no better place to do it.

Coming home to the empty enclosures was awful. Little Rhondda was a ghost town. All I had left was Amy. She was in fine health but did not show any overt pleasure on seeing me return.

"Yeah, whatever. You're back, then?"

Chimps will always make a great fuss when I return now from an overseas trip, but Amy has always been more pragmatic.

"Great to see you. Now where's my dinner?"

Robin and Mary had done a good job in looking after her. Then Robin Dunham offered me a lifeline by fixing me up with a temporary job on the maintenance staff at Chessington. I was grateful, but when I was given the task of making fibreglass rubbish bins in the shape of gorillas, I hit the lowest point of all and it made me realise how things had changed.

I spoke to Jim, but the reality of Monkey World was still a million miles away. Nevertheless, I realised that, despite our manifold differences, we were cut from the same cloth. Like me, Jim operated best when up against it and, while he encountered many troughs, he never had any doubt that his vision would become a reality.

I travelled around numerous zoos looking for work. I took Amy with me and hoped that the fact that I came with a valuable female orang-utan would open up some doors. It didn't.

"What are we going to do, old girl?" I asked her on the way back from the last trip made in vain.

In this state of flux and low spirits, I was happy to help when Jim rang with a proposition. In his role as head of small primates at Howletts, he had secured five douc langurs from a dealer in Rome. These rare and delicate leaf-eating monkeys were awaiting import licences in Italy, and Jim wanted me to go out and look after them while the wheels of bureaucracy creaked into motion. The delay meant they were in danger since Jim did not trust the dealer to deliver the specialised diet they needed. I agreed, but the deal was that Jim would look after Amy in return. Robin gave me leave from my fibreglass chore and I flew out the same day.

I did not know it at the time but Amy's peculiarities soon left Jim at the end of his tether and so he did what he always did so well on such occasions – he delegated. Several people helped and, together, they managed to get through. It was Amy's bloody-minded nature that drove people to distraction. Say one thing and she would do the opposite. It was as if she was playing an elaborate game with us all. Maybe she was.

Deciding to keep her was always a huge commitment, especially as I was adamant that she would not be a pet, but I felt I owed it to her somehow. I could have given her away, but the responsibility for her future lay with me. I wished I could have done the same for Horace but that was simply not possible. Now I was not going to lose another friend. I was separated from my wife and son, and had nowhere to live, but Amy was something tangible, something solid. While she hung onto me with her elongated fingers, I was also clinging onto her.

I spent six weeks in Rome while Jim worked to cut through the red tape. I rarely went out. I lived in a shabby motel next door to a noisy motorway. The windows rattled and were repeatedly lit up by passing headlights. It was a grim place but it suited my frame of mind. I have to admit I was not a very friendly person to know at this time and I had no interest in seeing the sights. I was there to do a job and wallowed in that and my own misery. I went to the dealer's house every day and ensured the langurs had the right diet, knowing full well that the wrong piece of fruit could be enough to kill them.

The monkeys, at least, thrived, which was no mean achievement, as one tiny female had not been able to stand when I arrived, but I was dragged to new depths of despair by my stay in Italy. With too much time on my hands, I thought long and hard about my personal situation.

On my return to England, I took a job at Howletts. At first I was still living on Gordon's estate and commuted the 80 miles from Weybridge every day. Each morning, Amy and I would rise early and I would give her some breakfast. Then we would go to the car and drive to the zoo in the old VW Passat I had spent my £1,000 redundancy money on. Money was so tight that I could only afford third-party insurance.

John Aspinall allowed me to keep Amy in Howletts' fruit shed while I carried out my duties. I made a small living area for her and she was happy to stay there. Some of the other keepers would come in to say hello, but I was conscious of not abusing my position and I wanted Amy to keep a low profile. She was still less than a year old and she weighed just six kilos. I looked at her one day and said: "I thought you were meant to be a great ape." She glared back at me and I almost expected a clip around the ear.

The commute was a pain in the neck, but I knew I'd be lucky to get a caravan to live in if I moved to Howletts. Anyway, I always viewed the job there as a stopgap because, although they boasted a splendid collection of monkeys, my primary interest was the orang and, hence, I was never really fulfilled there. I did not even bother to unpack.

After a few weeks, an ex-council house opposite the zoo became available. I moved in with Amy, Ermentrude the python and my collection of birds of prey. I was still sad that my marriage to Gill had failed, but was focused on Amy and Jim. We still spoke incessantly about what he always termed his pipe dream.

"Can we stop dreaming and start living?" I said to him.

"It won't be long," he said. "I've found the perfect site."

"Where is it?"

"A disused pig farm in Dorset."

It did not sound promising.

"The only trouble is getting planning permission."

"Right."

"And the highways. They want another road putting in."

"I see."

"I'll sort it. Don't worry."

"Okay. I'll sithee."

I went along with him as achieving the impossible is always an attractive proposition, but we still seemed to be nowhere near bringing our dreams to fruition.

That night, I got Amy from the fruit shed and we walked to the car. I picked up Meryl and we went to her parents' in Walton-on-Thames. Then I got Jamie from his mother's for one of his regular visits. Amy, as ever, was sitting in my lap. I hesitate to mention that now, but it seemed the most sensible way of travelling with a very dependent orang-utan. I remember driving along the M2 towards Kent. It was 11.30pm. Then I fell asleep and everything went black.

8

The Crash

PHIL WAS A big, burly policeman who had seen it all. At least he thought he had until he got to the scene on the M2 near Faversham and heard the woman screaming about an orang-utan. He looked at the upturned car and noted it had been scrunched up as if it were bacon foil. He reasoned that he could not wait for the ambulance. This was a bad one. So he ignored the shattered glass on the ground and began to edge his way into the rear of the car. He was expecting the worst, but he was not expecting the sight of a hairy, non-human hand wrapped around my red head.

Phil was terrified of animals. And this was

something beyond his comprehension. It was clearly some sort of big monkey. Maybe an ape. Whatever it was, man and beast were both upside down in a perilous situation. As well as the seriousness of the crash and the obvious injuries, the possibility of another vehicle ploughing into the car worried Phil. So he swallowed his fear and pulled me and Amy out of the car.

Meryl was unhurt and Jamie only bruised. They had been lucky. The screech of the siren and winking blue flash signalled the arrival of the ambulance. Amy and I were both put in the back. I was unconscious and she was subdued. Like me, she had received a bang on the head and she was hurt and frightened. I can only imagine the puzzled faces of those who saw us being rushed down the corridors of the Kent and Canterbury Hospital. And the faces of the doctors.

Luckily, the SOS call had gone out to Jim and he arrived soon afterwards. He looked at me and must have had a terrible feeling of déjà vu. His good friend Bob Wilson had already been killed by a tiger while performing his duties at Howletts and now he thought I was on my way out too. He had already told me that I was the only person who had faith in what he was doing. Now the duty consultant examined me and said he did not think I would make it through the night. Crestfallen, Jim turned his attention to Amy. She was more lucid but had still suffered a nasty bang on the head. Jim took her off to see Ken Pack, the Howletts vet, while my parents were called. I was rushed to intensive care in a coma. The hospital called my mother to tell her the grave news.

"I'm afraid your son is unlikely to live until morning," the consultant said down the phone. "He is clinically brain dead."

My mother hid her emotions well. "He's never been brain alive," she replied, before giving her permission to turn off the life support machine. "I do not agree with keeping people alive in a vegetative state," she said. "A waste of resources."

Of course, all of this was relayed to me much later. Luckily, the consultant delayed heeding her advice and others were more sympathetic. Robin Dunham was in an important management meeting at Chessington World of Adventures when the news came in. He dropped everything and sped to my bedside. Later, he would send me a card with the message: "Death is nature's way of telling you to slow down." Make of that what you will, but it certainly made me laugh when I was well enough to read it.

Jim also camped out in the hospital and his work back at the zoo was neglected as a result. The accident happened on Wednesday night and I finally came out of the coma at noon on the Saturday. My father and grandmother came to see me, but my mother never bothered. Knowing I am a relentless diarist, Meryl filled in the blank days in my notebook on my behalf:

Wednesday, August 8:
Car accident on M2 outside Faversham at
11.30pm. Jeremy, Jamie, Meryl and Amy
taken to Kent and Canterbury Hospital.
Jeremy in coma. Everyone else okay.

Thursday, August 9: Jeremy in coma.

Friday, August 10: Jeremy in coma.

Saturday, August 11: Jeremy out of coma at midday.

Sunday, August 12: Jeremy in ITU.

Monday, August 13: Jeremy in ITU.

Tuesday, August 14: Jeremy in ITU.

Wednesday, August 15: Jeremy in ITU.

Thursday, August 16: Jeremy moved to ward.

Saturday, September 1: Jeremy home for the weekend (Littlebourne opposite Howletts).

Sunday, September 2: Jeremy home. Jim and Meryl took Jeremy back to hospital 7pm.

Tuesday, September 4: Jeremy home to Littlebourne.

No other diary entries were made for 1984.

During my incarceration in hospital, I did manage to escape and the police found me wandering the streets of Canterbury in a surgical gown and with my catheter bag attached.

"Come on, sir, let's get back to the hospital," one said kindly.

"I am looking for capuchin monkeys," I replied. "They've escaped."

"Monkeys?"

"Yes, now are you going to help me catch them or not?"

I was not in good health. I was returned to my bed and placed under greater scrutiny. At one point, both Gill, my ex-wife, and Meryl, my now girlfriend, were at my bedside together. I think I may have been pretending to be unconscious at that point.

As things improved, I started to read *Jonathan Livingston Seagull*, Richard Bach's fable about a bird and the need to find a higher purpose, which I found helped me. Most of all, I was glad to be reunited with Amy. She had suffered a nasty blow to the head and had apparently been particularly miserable for a few days before getting back to normal.

My recovery from the crash took a very long time and nothing would truly look the same thereafter. There is no doubt that it gave me a wider perspective. I read Bach, hugged Amy and came to appreciate the basic values and relationships that sometimes get taken for granted. With this attitude it is possible to gain something positive from even the bleakest of situations.

I had fractured my skull in three places and there was a fragmented area above my right ear. The medic imparted this knowledge in such a sombre manner that he became known as Dr Grim. Indeed, whenever anybody asked, "What are his prospects?" that was his one-word reply. As I recuperated, I reverted to my regular health professional, Dr Bliss, which was her real name. I now think that this combination, Dr Grim and Dr Bliss, is the perfect summary of a fight for survival. It is a bittersweet balancing act.

Jim and I rarely showed much emotion to each other. He was too busy dreaming his dream, while I was hanging onto his coat-tails and fending for Amy. But one day, while still in hospital, Jim arrived at my bedside and he let his guard down. He held my hand and said, "Come on, Jeremy, I'm not going to lose you."

I was barely conscious at that point, but the words still shocked me.

"I've lost Bob and I'm not going to lose another friend."

The strength I gained from Jim letting his mask slip momentarily was enormous.

Jim started taking me to the zoo for therapy. I really must have looked quite something because the surgeons had shaved my hair and the wound was still a gruesome sight. I grew tired very quickly, but as time went on, my strength returned and I relished being around animals again. The only problem was that Dr

Bliss was taking a leaf from Dr Grim's book and refused to sign the document which would enable me to return to work full-time. All my entreaties were greeted with the same emphatic no.

This meant that I was working a full week but had to exist on statutory sick pay. It was tough but, luckily, when Dr Bliss was away one day, a locum took her place and, unused to people asking to go back to work rather than be signed off, he fell into my trap and signed the form. Dr Bliss was most irritated when she returned, but realised I was not for turning. Her attitude was well intentioned, however, and a later scan showed that I had, indeed, suffered significant brain damage in the accident.

The next three years would be a hazy recuperation period. Meryl and I married and had a son, Kenyon, but I have to confess I have vague recollections from that time. I was deputy to Jim at Howletts, but the days merged into one and I suffered memory loss and crippling headaches. It was a half-life, with the long-term effect being the loss of my sense of smell, although in my chosen profession that was, perhaps, something of a blessing.

One day that has remained in my mind was that Boxing Day, 1984. The air was chill that morning and my breath turned to cold smoke. A thick frost dusted the zoo and I pulled my hood close around my face as I ventured out into the gale. Toto, one of the old bull elephants, was also struggling and took a nasty tumble on the ice. John Aspinall, the idiosyncratic owner and a man to be feared, was present with a phalanx of Boxing Day guests, and they all joined us in trying to manhandle Toto back to his feet. It was to no avail.

"Hang on," one of the keepers piped. "There's a forklift down by the tiger house. That could help."

"We haven't got a driver," Mr A responded.

I didn't hesitate. "Don't worry about that," I said. "I'll sort it out."

Me and my big mouth. I had absolutely no experience of operating a forklift, but, as I have said, necessity is the mother of invention and I wondered how hard it could be. I found the old, rusting truck and quickly hot-wired it, the years of working with Barker's bangers bearing fruit. By the time I had gained a rudimentary grasp of the controls, I had already demolished one safety barrier and alarmed a good number of visitors. I pressed on and managed to get the forks under Toto and helped lift him slowly back to his feet. Once he felt terra firma, he did a little jig and turned quickly around, scattering most of the watching crew.

Alas, Mr A and his esteemed guests found themselves trapped and had no escape. As Toto walked towards them, they had no choice but to edge backwards. Back and into the dirty, icy pond, which was a foul shade of green. Their finery was soon wrecked, but they later joined in our mirth at the sight. Toto seemed good as new and I spent the afternoon repairing the trail of devastation I had left in my wake. These things were sent to try us, I suppose. It was just that they were sent with alarming regularity. I was still regarded as something of a tough individual by some of my co-workers at that time, but it wasn't really me. Underneath I was as soft as putty and I think they began to appreciate that when all the macho keepers would congregate in the café, while I sat in the corner knitting Jamie a Dennis the Menace jumper.

It was a period of sketchy uncertainty, but Amy, as ever, was something of a rock. She had now outgrown the small accommodation quarters I had built for her in the house, so I set about constructing something better on the patio. Even though she would still accompany me as I rode my bicycle around, her long, matted hair and rubber hand occasionally obscuring my vision and putting us both in fresh peril, my intention was always to see Amy living with other animals.

"I like you, dear," I told her one day, "but don't you think you should start behaving like an orang-utan?"

She was nonplussed by such barbs and was probably unaware that she was one. To her, I was her mother; an odd-looking, gruff mother, perhaps, but a mother nonetheless.

I deliberately ensured that the new steel cage was precisely the right size to be transported on Steve Matthews' truck. Steve was a builder-cum-timber merchant and was Jim's partner in those early days and, together, we took a trip down to see the site in Dorset that Jim had found. Steve had suggested we drive down in his splendid new car, a Lotus Esprit, but it failed to start when we gathered at 5am, so my trusty but ancient VW Polo was pressed into service.

Both Steve and I had been press-ganged into housing many of the monkeys that Jim was stockpiling from various laboratories. Every Friday, I would corner Jim and literally force him to empty his pockets of 50-pence pieces, which I would then use to feed the electricity meter in my garden shed to maintain the precise 20-degree temperature needed for the band of small primates living there. Steve, too, had converted his house into a mini zoo and had around 40 monkeys. Every day after work, I would make the eight-mile trip to Steve's house to feed his guests and ensure everybody was happy.

Jim also had some refugees at his place for a while. That was why the emergency call came through one wintry day.

"I'm snowed in, Jeremy," Jim said with a degree of panic, "and the monkeys are out of food."

"Don't worry," I told him. "I'll sort it out."

The thick waves of snow meant it was treacherous on the roads, but I knew we had to feed our chaps. And so, against zoo policy, I wandered down to the big cat section and borrowed a Land Rover to negotiate the six miles to Chateau Cronin. Being used to my ailing VW, I assumed the Land Rover could cope with any weather, but suddenly I heard a slush and a thud and we came to a very definite stop. The blizzard quickly formed a blanket on the windscreen. I struggled out into the knee-deep snow and realised I was well and truly stuck.

I decided the first thing to do was deliver the food, so I slung the sack on my back and began the arduous journey to Jim's, stumbling, sliding and swearing as I went. Jim was relieved and I made light of my situation, assuming I could move the stricken Land Rover with a bit of luck. Alas, when I returned, I found the vehicle to be far less mobile than Toto the horizontal elephant. The snowdrift appeared to be sucking the Land Rover down into the ground, so I set about trying to dig it out with my bare hands. I felt like King Canute, as more snow fell, but finally, after three hours, and with a frostbitten ear and mounting regret at having taken a zoo vehicle without permission, I was free. It was well after midnight by the time home was lit up by my headlights and I fell through the door like a latter-day Captain Oates. Meryl stirred when I climbed into bed. "Oh, I wondered where you'd gone," she said before going back to sleep.

That sensation of being stuck applied to other areas as our pipe dream survived by a thread. It was a rollercoaster ride as Jim pursued finances and planning permission with a zealous vigour. It was hard. People were sceptical and the locals, understandably, were concerned by the thought of a bunch of wild animals suddenly moving in next door. One minute we thought we were making inroads and the next there would be another setback. We lived in limbo and I was held together only by Amy's companionship and Jim's incredible passion.

I wandered into the café at Howletts one day and found the care staff in the throes of a great debate.

"Sit down, Jeremy," Jim implored. "We're trying to think of a name."

Camelot and Never-Never Land sprang to mind, but I kept my counsel.

"What about Monkey World?" someone suggested.

"That's good," Jim said. "Simple."

"Nah, I don't like it," I said. "It's too similar to Bird World in Surrey."

"Well, what do you suggest, then?"

I have to confess I could not come up with anything better and so, over a cold cup of coffee in a wooden shack at Howletts, Monkey World was born.

Jim was a maelstrom of energy as he waited for the planning verdict. It did not look good when the case went to appeal, but he put on his best suit and tie and made the trip down to Dorset for what he knew was make or break.

I stayed up in Kent and was feeding Amy when the phone rang. I knew it was Jim with the verdict. I looked at the big orange lump and wondered fleetingly how our lives might change in the next few seconds.

I picked up the phone and did not have to wait long.

"We got it!" Jim shouted. "We got it!"

I put down the receiver and walked to the fridge.

Then I drove down to Jim's house and left the bottle of champagne on his doorstep. Attached was a brief hand-written note: "We can do it!"

9

First Day

JIM QUIT HIS job at Howletts in the autumn of 1986 to concentrate on turning the dream into reality. I took over his role as head of small primates and things began to move on apace. My father-in-law, Barry McCaully, was a well-connected London lawyer, and introduced Jim to various people with deep pockets, with a view to gaining the necessary funds. One of his contacts was Richard Pickance, an accountant who became another partner in Monkey World. It was now a race against time because the money-lenders had vowed to pull the plug on the entire project if we were not open by the following summer.

It nearly didn't get that far. I had a call from George Jacobs, a former keeper at Howletts, who was touring the UK with an elephant in an effort to get sponsorship to undertake a trans-Alps trek in the footsteps of Hannibal. Lola – the elephant – had fallen sick and George wondered if Jim was in Dorset, as he needed somewhere to rest her for a while as she got her health back. Jim, of course, agreed to help out his old colleague and so George turned up with Lola in his trailer. Jim arranged for a vet to come and check out the pachyderm, but the goodwill favour bit him on the backside when Lola died soon afterwards.

That was distressing enough, but suddenly a rumour began spreading that the cause of death had been anthrax. It was very hard to stifle gossip when it concerned something that was potentially devastating to the local farmers. We also had a river running through the site, providing water to a number of local farms, and so it would have been easy for the disease to spread. The truth, of course, was very different and it was not hard to prove that Lola had been ill and had a number of health issues, but the local community was still worried. People are naturally suspicious of anything new and this was an inauspicious start. Confidence in us was not running high and if I'd been the owner of a prize herd of cattle, I would have felt the same. Luckily, Jim always came into his own when backed into a corner and he stressed the facts to the local press. He told them that it was a terribly sad event, but Lola's death could not have had any knock-on effect. Nevertheless, it was yet another hurdle to overcome.

In 1986 Gordon Mills passed away and I went to his funeral, a suitably star-studded affair, and I met the likes of Tom Jones for the first time. I will always be grateful to Gordon for giving me the chance to work with such a fantastic collection of animals, especially the orangs, and the freedom he afforded me.

It was also a wonderful place for the kids. Working so closely with animals may not have helped married life, but it meant my children had a magical playground. Kenyon was growing and Jamie also returned to live with me. My separation from Gill had grown less amicable as Jamie grew older and lost his dependency on his mother. Gill even took me to the Child Support Agency, claiming I owed her more money. They told her I was actually paying too much and that she would be better off keeping quiet. Eventually, when Gill got a new boyfriend, Jamie rang and said he wanted to come and live with me. I had always told him that it would only take a call but it had to come from him. Gill, unsurprisingly, was not happy and delivered several abusive phone calls to me, which Meryl usually ended up fielding. I like to think I have always done what I can for the kids. I have never pushed them into anything and have let them go their own way and make their own mistakes. That's how animals learn. As long as my children were happy and not living off others, then they were okay with me. Some parents may be stricter. Some, for instance, may not like it if their son has dreadlocks; I would just be jealous that I couldn't grow them myself.

The following January, in 1987, Meryl fell pregnant again. I was delighted, but it meant we were entering the unknown, with no guarantee of an income and with a baby on the way. Soon afterwards, the time came for Amy's cage to be shifted to Dorset. Steve turned up in his truck and we tried to lift the cage onto the back. To my horror, the carefully worked-out specifications were all wrong and the cage was a few feet too wide. I cursed Steve and his truck. Then, with the heaviest of hearts, I took out my angle grinder and carved my labour of love into sections. Crestfallen, I then loaded it onto the back of the truck and watched it disappear into the distance. It is fair to say the omens were bleak. Amy, meanwhile, was oblivious and delighted to have the run of the house again, sleeping in a box in the kitchen and generally doing as she pleased.

A few days later, it was our turn to leave. I was excited and wondered what Steve had done with the corrugated iron hut that he had promised to transform into a lovely new home.

"We're going to do it up lovely," he had told me. "Line the walls, put a nice floor down, make it a real palace."

"Whatever, Steve," I had told him. "As long as it's dry and there's enough room for me, the family and Amy. That's all I want."

I called Ken Pack, the Howletts vet, and he came down and sedated Amy. She had been used to travelling around in cars, but she was getting older and was quite big now. I had not taken her anywhere in the car for some time, as part of my grand plan to get her to behave like an orang-utan and not a house pet. We put her in the car and Sian, Meryl's sister, nursed her during the four-hour trip. I kept an eye on them both in the mirror, as well as the overloaded trailer swaying behind us. Meryl, her mother, Jamie and Kenyon went in the other car.

We arrived to find a bomb-site. Steve had only just started stripping the walls of our iron shack. The supposed two-bedroom extension was a dilapidated mobile home several metres away, pockmarked with moss and damp. Amy's cage, once painstakingly put together by me, was now a metal mess piled on the floor amid the debris. I considered my situation. I had a pregnant wife, a sedated orang-utan, a trailer full of furniture and a half-built shed. Jim, curiously, was nowhere to be found, probably because he realised how behind schedule we were and thought it best to hide from me for a while.

"What do you think?" Steve asked.

"Are you serious?"

We went inside and I noticed a dark brown imitation wood that was as foul as it was depressing. "We can't live in this."

It was quickly decided that Meryl and Kenyon would go back with her mother to stay in Surrey while I got the place habitable. In the meantime, Amy and I stayed in the creaking mobile home, me wondering quite what we had got ourselves into and Amy no doubt wondering when I was going to get around to giving her something to eat.

There was no time for self-pity and I toiled like a man possessed the following day. Amy sat and watched as I worked away at her cage. I could almost hear her thinking, "What's the idiot up to now?"

It was two days before the first shipment of ring-tailed lemurs requiring quarantine accommodation arrived from a science laboratory. There were a few disused barns on the site, but nothing else. Once I had Amy's cage up and running, I set about creating something for the lemurs. In my haste to get an enclosure ready for our guests, I had left no way of shutting off the lemurs while I cleaned their cage. This would not normally be a problem because lemurs are no more destructive than your average house cat, but I knew that one of the males, whom I had christened Gunga Din, came with a particularly nasty reputation. Faced with no choice, I entered the cage and gave Gunga Din the benefit of the doubt. Unfortunately, he was less forgiving and, as soon as I entered his space, he jumped onto my shoulders and sank his teeth deep into my back and hand.

"Aaaahhhhh!"

The pain was awful and so, on my second day at Monkey World, I made the first of many trips to the local hospital to be stitched back together.

Jim arrived the following week with his wife, Roz, and daughter, Eleanor. It is a sign of the struggle we faced in those early days that I had actually lent Jim the money to buy an engagement ring. It was good to see him because we were now frantically trying to get everything ready for the big opening in August. We had to prove that we had a viable business this summer or we were done for, and it didn't look promising.

One of the main attractions for the punters was to be nine chimpanzees rescued from Spain. Jim had committed to taking the chimps from an ex-pat couple named Simon and Peggy Templer, who had been appalled at the trade of smuggling baby apes from Africa to work with beach photographers. The Templers had rescued the chimps and they had lived with various other primates in the spacious garden of their Barcelona home. They had also become involved with Ken Pack, who was now another partner in Monkey World, and it was Ken who realised it would benefit all parties if we took some of the Templer chimps. It was a great idea, apart from the fact that we could not get quarantine approval for their new two-acre enclosure in time, so to placate the planning department, a chimpanzee house far surpassing the necessary security specifications was prefabricated in Kent and trucked down in flat-pack form for us to assemble.

We converted the barns into homes for the many

ex-lab monkeys that we were acquiring all the time, including marmosets, tamarins, douroucoulis, squirrel monkeys, vervets and crab-eating macaques, as well as six sub-species of lemur. I made contact with a string of wholesale greengrocers to provide the food for our rapidly expanding family, and set up accounts for bedding, bowls and cleaning tools. The race was on.

The arrivals were only part of the equation, however, and we had teething trouble with unexpected departures too. The first to go was one of our anouchis, a huge South American relative of the guinea pig. Embarrassingly, the rodent got out within minutes of arriving, but luckily for us, he stayed in the locality and I devised a trap. Within a few days, he was back with his mate.

I then hired a van to pick up four wallabies from Whipsnade Safari Park. The intention was for them to roam freely around the exhibits, but not quite as freely as they had in mind as they merrily scampered off to explore the wilds of Dorset. Nobody has ever been savaged by a wallaby and they have lived feral in North Yorkshire for decades, but the occasional sightings of them did little to bolster our fragile relationship with the locals, who still remembered the sad tale of Lola the elephant and the anthrax rumours.

We were lucky that the wallabies, because of their time at Whipsnade, were not fearful of man and so did not disappear for long. A farmer rang the park and said he had seen them, so I gathered a net and drove over to his place. The farmer looked decidedly unimpressed by events, but stoically helped me net the wallabies. The bad publicity was the last thing we needed and I therefore decided the best thing to do would be to rehome them before they caused more problems. They were soon despatched to Sussex.

Although our subsequent record with escapees has been excellent, the wallabies were sadly not the last to make a bid for freedom in those early days. Jim's wife had a pair of raccoons and one of them, Rocky, also went missing. His exile lasted a fortnight, during which there were numerous sightings of a masked bandit within a one-mile radius. I was well aware that a raccoon could live quite happily in the surrounding woods for evermore, but reassured Jim that he would come home soon.

"Look, I'll make it worth your while," he told me one night. "If you get him back, I'll give you a tenner."

These bargains were made over most of the escapees and I later had to remind Jim of them. However, there was a serious side to it and, with local disapproval festering, we needed Rocky back. Once again, I took out my welder and devised a cunning trap. I knew he would return if he got hungry; so I baited the trap with a piece of meat and put the contraption close to where he had left. Sure enough, it was not long before Rocky sniffed his dinner, stood on the metal plate and the door slammed shut. I never saw the tenner, but it was still worth it in terms of the bad press avoided.

Three weeks before opening day, we received our first batch of chimps from Simon and Peggy Templer. It was past midnight when the headlights of a truck heralded their arrival and they lumbered into the park. Unable to use their vast enclosure because of the quarantine restrictions, I had set about welding them a makeshift cage. I am proud to say that the cage is still used as a "temporary" enclosure today.

The problems and histories of the first batch of chimps were both typical and depressing. Paddy was the dominant male, aloof and wary of human contact, but he was kind and in a good physical condition compared with some of his travelling companions. They included Beth, who was missing four toes from her right foot, the result of being shot or snared in the wild, and who arrived with infections and suffering from malnutrition.

Then there was Zoe. She constantly sucked her cheeks, which was probably the result of being snatched from the wild before being fully weaned, and Cindy, who had trouble walking after being made to wear sandals in her role as a beach photographer's prop. Busta was also part of this group. A photographer's aid by day, he was made to work in the circus by night and consequently was quiet and very aggressive at first. I quickly realised he had infected teeth and, when our dentist had fixed them, he became a much more placid chap.

The days passed in a frenzy of activity. Steve worked on landscaping and I recall there was a lot of finger-pointing and disagreements. Jim and Steve would be in the throes of a discussion about where each tree should go, while I raised my eyebrows and just got on with it. This was highlighted when Steve bought an ancient Hymac digger which was reliable only in its inconsistency.

"Er, do you know how to put a track on a digger?" Steve asked one day when he was using it to dig out a pond and had become stuck.

"No, but I can find out."

Finally, it was August 6, the night before what threatened to be a not very grand opening. It had already been an epic journey. Jim and I both looked frazzled as we sat down over a cup of tea. There was no sense of satisfaction, just fear of what tomorrow would bring and the daunting realisation that we were not ready.

"Well, this is it," Jim said.

"I guess so."

"I told you we'd do it."

"Never in doubt."

We afforded each other a wry smile as we went off to our beds, wondering if anyone would turn up and whether we would see out the summer.

The gentle daybreak was pierced by the noise of our newcomers and nagging doubts. I busied myself with my normal routine and had breakfast with Amy.

"What do you think, old girl?" I asked.

She held her fruit in her hand and sniffed it suspiciously. It was one of the occasions when I thought the simplicity of an orang-utan life would suit me just fine, revolving chiefly around food and procreation. I lifted the frayed curtain edge and looked through a cracked window pane to the outside world. The future was almost here.

Jim had worked a miracle to get us to this point, but it was all held together by shoestrings and Band-Aids. He was the consummate politician – his comic as a child had been the *New Statesman* – and this was his cause. I genuinely think the reason Jim did not like being in America was that he was just another American there. In his own way, he had more in common with the typical English eccentric like John Aspinall. He came here and he was someone. And Monkey World was his masterpiece.

Except you would not have known it from the first day. My diary entry that night, August 7, 1987, was blunt and to the point. "Various public unhappy."

To be honest, for all our best efforts, you could not blame them. The main problem was most of our monkeys had been rescued from laboratories and, having spent their lives living in confined spaces, they were hesitant about exploring their vast, new enclosures.

"What's up with them?" Steve asked as we stood outside the crab-eating macaques' enclosure, squinting into the emptiness in the hope of seeing something.

"They're agoraphobic," I muttered.

"Brilliant."

The watching public were not slow to voice their disapproval.

"What a load of rubbish!" huffed one gorilla of a man. "It's a bleeding con." Others nodded their heads in agreement.

I sighed. If you have lived in a two-foot cube for your whole life, the fact is you do not suddenly rush outside screaming, "Eureka!" So the monkeys stayed indoors, while the lemurs ran up the trees and stayed there. In time we would learn much about the behaviour of lab animals. We found out, for instance, that if a monkey is happy, he simply does not want to go outside. Leave a door open and his first thought will be, "It's dangerous out there, sod that." Others will just think, "I'll stay here, thanks very much." We have a policy never to lock our animals outside, despite the size of their enclosures, because we know they like their security.

Our survival depended on our takings and it was clear that word of mouth was not going to be particularly favourable. Our timid refugees and more forthright punters made for an ill-fated mix.

"This doesn't look good," Jim said when we convened at lunchtime.

"Moaning sods," Steve commented.

"Moaning sods, perhaps, but they're our livelihood," Jim added.

We watched one group of people shuffling between the apparently empty enclosures and looking up at the lemurs' trees, mystified. We could sense the dissatisfaction. Then a light bulb flashed.

"Hang on a minute," I said.

"What?"

"I've got an idea. I'll be five minutes."

With that, I rushed back to my corrugated-iron shack and lifted the latch.

"Right, old girl," I said. "It's showtime."

Amy looked more disgruntled than the most bitter of guests.

"Come on," I implored her. "I need your help."

I took her by the hand and she jumped up onto my chest, wrapping one huge, leathery hand tightly under my arm. She was getting bigger now, and I wanted her to become more independent, but needs must. We wandered out into the park and we shuffled along until we came across the first batch of guests. The reaction was instant. Eyes lit up and the children cracked smiles. The result was that the parents were placated.

"This is Amy," I began and I gave a talk about orang-utans and this one's particular quirks. It was a long speech.

"She's so cute," a woman gushed.

Amy would have been unimpressed by such compliments and I felt like telling the truth. About how she could actually be the most awkward of animals, how they would not think her cute if they had hand-reared her, and that while it may be bad having to change a baby's nappy, they should try doing it with an orangutan and its hairy backside. That may challenge any view on conservation.

Amy, though, was a huge hit. I squeezed her and she tapped me on the head with her knuckles, as if to see if there was anything inside. Buoyed by the rescue mission, I ran back to the hut with Amy, deposited her in her living area and picked up Ermentrude, my python. I wrapped her around my neck and returned for another interactive talk. There were more questions, although Amy was clearly the favourite, and then I made one last quick change, returning with an injured buzzard I had rescued and nurtured. As I told the crowd of his terrible plight, he dutifully pulled faces at the spectators to wring the last vestiges of sympathy from them.

When the guests began to leave, I loitered by the gate and listened to their comments. They were not exactly brimming over with enthusiasm, but they no longer felt they had been robbed. Albert's bouncy castle and burger van helped too. We were up and, although running would be stretching it, we were at least stumbling along on a broken buzzard wing and a prayer.

It was late by the time I returned to my hut. The moon

lit the cracks between the trees and I felt a brief moment of contentment. The apes and monkeys were all tucked up inside. Back at home Amy wrapped her arms around herself and sat in the corner like an oversized gonk, unaware of what she had done. I smiled and gave her some milk. Not for the first time in my life, Amy had saved the day.

10

Amy Makes a Friend

MERYL'S LABOUR STARTED at 1am but, as the contractions were only mild, I hastened to work and made sure I cared for the animals. Luckily, the more severe contractions waited until 6pm, by which time all the beasts were tucked up for the night. I went back to the hospital, but was assured by the doctors that nothing was going to happen that night and so was booted out at 9pm.

I refer to my diary entry for the following day, October 4, 1987:

Started work at 5.30am. Got all the cleaning and

feeding done by 9am. Just left Jim to give the chimps their lunch and then put them to bed with supper. Didn't clean the tamarin shed but should be okay. Left for hospital at 9.30am. Took till 5.30pm for Megan to be born. Seems okay. Got home 7ish. Saw to all my animals and Jim's cock-ups.

On reading that, my current and best wife, Lou, told me she would have summarily killed me had she been around then.

The park was now closed during the week. We had survived the first summer but it was an insecure existence and we waged constant battles against bureaucracy and nature. Just a matter of days after Megan was born, a hurricane ripped through the south, wreaking havoc and causing carnage. Two firemen were killed in Dorset as trees were uprooted and buildings demolished. We were lucky. Steve had carefully planned the layout of the park so that no trees would be a danger to any of the buildings or enclosures. I gave Megan a kiss and set about making sure the rest of my family was all right. I was relieved to find there was only minor damage to the buildings, as the fact of the matter was we simply didn't have the money to replace them.

I realised things were okay when I saw Paddy and his band of chimps darting around their enclosure as if nothing had happened. Paddy was still a somewhat distant figure and suspicious of humans. He did not want or need social contact with me, which suited me fine because that made him a better chimp. A lot of animals in captivity, particularly rescued or abused ones, become dependent on humans. Paddy was always above that sort of thing and it would be months and months before we had any physical contact. In those early days of our relationship, he was still indulging in a macho routine, beating his chest and hollering regular warnings. Chimps, it is fair to say, are very like humans in their insecurities. A big male will want to throw someone around to assert his dominance and Paddy only really accepted me when he realised I was not after his women.

It was a big thrill for me to go in with him and his group that first winter. I made sure I came across as passive and non-confrontational because Paddy's instinct was to say, "What the hell are you doing in here?" I pandered to his vanity and spoke to him softly.

"Gosh, I think you're a marvellous chap."

"Yes, you're really very strong."

It was an adventure. Each member of Paddy's band

was different and I bonded with some more quickly than others. The natural way for a chimp to show acceptance is to give you the finger – in a nice way. You then take it in your mouth before repeating the gesture. It may not sound too daunting, but chimps can be sneaky and putting your finger in an animal's mouth is always a risk. It would be over a year before I got to that stage with Paddy. Finally, he did let me, but it was always done in a secretive way, when nobody else was looking. He was the same with the other chimps. He would be happy to sit around and chew the fat with an individual, but if others came along he would revert to being the great leader. Orangs, I am glad to say, do not bother with all of this. They do have their own social tics, but they are incomparable and nowhere near as complex. You will get them living together in the wild, but it will be for security or because there is fruit on those trees, not for family reasons. Their hierarchy largely begins and ends with a mother and baby bonding by necessity, as Amy and I had done. However, I did not want Amy to become reliant on me, so I ended up being cruel to be kind. I knew Amy's gene pool was too valuable to waste. I wanted her to live with other orangs and, one day, be a mother.

Unfortunately, she did not behave much like an

orang-utan at all. She had breakfast with Kenyon and would sit on his bed, next to his gorilla soft toy. One day, I decided enough was enough and thought I would turn her into the real deal. So I took her outside and showed her the trees that surrounded our hut.

"This," I said as I pointed upwards, "is known as a tree. You climb them."

Amy looked unimpressed. She hung onto me and showed no natural inclination to start shinning up the trunk. I sighed. There was only one thing for it and so, with an air of weary inevitability, I started climbing the tree with her attached. When we got to the top, I hoped she would disembark and do what orangs do. Instead, she clung onto me and was not for moving. I managed to prise her off me and deposited her at the top of the tree before climbing down quickly. I had barely got to the bottom before the screaming began. I raised my eyebrows as the noise grew louder and started climbing back up. I imagine I am the only man to have saved an orang-utan from a tree. She jumped back onto me and I fixed her with an incredulous glare.

"How come I get the only orang-utan in the world who is scared of heights?" I asked. It shows that only some of what animals do is instinct; the rest is learnt by example. It was only much later, when Amy got her own enclosure and when she thought I wasn't looking, that she decided she would happily climb to the highest point possible to see what was going on elsewhere. It was a point of principle with her. If I wanted her to do something, then she would do the opposite.

That first winter was dominated by trying to get our chaps used to their new enclosures. First up was Paddy. Jim's dream had always been to defy the cynics by confining our chimps using electric fences. It would be a milestone in British zoological history if it worked, but the naysayers were loud and plentiful. Jim was undaunted. The concept was to get away from the old image of wrought-iron cages, which gave the impression that the animals were being held in a prison against their will. We were a sanctuary and put the welfare of our animals ahead of everything. Making money was merely a means to survive and furnish the dream.

We knew we had to get Paddy's group used to the perils of the fence for it to work. The way we did this was by installing a dummy fence within the temporary cage that I had built. I then introduced the chimps to it. I fastened white tassels onto the wires as a visual aid so that they would remember that the thing hurt. Slowly, I removed two tassels a day until they were used to the idea that it was the wire that was the source of the painful jolt.

The fence we used was known as the Elephant II and had been developed to stop elephants from raiding maize fields in Africa. The technique was also used to confine cattle in Australia, as it was a cheap way of fencing in hundreds of miles of land. Nobody had done it with chimps, though. It was widely considered impossible.

On a farm where electric fences are used, the charge is 3,000 volts. We went up to 8,000 volts. That sounds very high by comparison, but the volts are actually the speed of the current. The thing that hurts is the amp and we measured ours in milliamps, or joules, which meant the charge was enough to give a little shock, but not enough to cause any real harm.

Some people considered what we were doing a risk, but we were professional and Jim had studied the science. The truth was we also had little choice because we were so short of money. Paddy learnt very quickly that if he left the fence alone, it would refrain from biting him. That was a big moment for us. Once he and his band were trained to the fence in the dummy cage, we erected 12-foot-high fences around their enclosure. These were a world away from the horrible iron cages of yore, though, and we felt pretty proud of ourselves by the time we had finished fencing in Paddy and his chums.

It was March by the time we were ready. Finally, eight months after we had first opened our gates, we had all the necessary papers. We felt like we were breaking down barriers by putting up fences. As I had been working so closely with Paddy's group, acclimatising them to the fence and working out their different characters, I went in first. I looked out at the watching faces. Jim was there and I wondered how he must have felt. This was his dream and the concept he had staked his reputation and money on. I saw Jane Goodall, the famous anthropologist, who had come down to witness such an historic moment. There was a smattering of oversized lenses and press people. The capacity for egg on our faces was huge.

The door of the chimps' quarters was slid open and the chaps bundled out. Nervously, they gathered around me for reassurance. Even Paddy seemed slightly fazed by the situation. I decided the best course of action would be to take them on a short tour of their facilities. We did, and Paddy soon decided that enough was enough. He took his group back inside and the moment was over. Jane Goodall was effusive. The flashbulbs went off. For once we were big news for the right reasons.

It would not be long before Paddy and Co settled into their enclosure, which they celebrated by merrily vandalising the assorted pine trees. That, in a nutshell, is the way chimps are. They love each other dearly but will rip each other apart, nevertheless. You might say they are like football hooligans. Everything is done to provoke a response. They can be proud and vain. The orang, by contrast, wouldn't even have a mirror.

Before the second summer, I got hold of a doomed MOT failure for free. It was only a Mini Traveller, disfigured by rust and bleached of colour, and it lacked doors and bonnet. Still, it proved a major asset in transporting things around the site until the day a year later when I overloaded it with steel bars and the suspension broke and it finally passed away.

Another more valuable arrival was my first assistant. Liz Miles came to us on a job creation scheme, which was backed by the government and so did not bite into our meagre finances.

"How do you like orang-utans?" I asked her.

"Er, I don't really know any," she answered.

"Well, we need to build a house for the one back in my shack."

It was time for Amy to have her own enclosure, rather

than a place with me or a cage tacked onto a patio. So Liz and I dug out the foundations ourselves and then laid the concrete base by hand. Once we had dug out the drainage ditch, we handed over to the real builders. That is one of the mantras I have developed from working in a world like this – know your limitations.

In early April 1988, the day came for Amy to move into her splendid new home. It was odd not to have her living with me, but I was happy that she was getting the chance to move on. People often think it must be terrible to say goodbye to an animal you have lived with, but if they knew the hardships involved, they might have a different opinion. Anyway, I could still see Amy every day and this had been my big ambition. I wanted to cast her out of the home so she could fend for herself. In time I hoped we would have lots of other orang-utans and Amy would become part of a natural world that she had never really known. So I settled her into her home and walked away, stopping to spy on her and see what she thought. Curiosity may have got the cat but it was never going to do for my girl. She sat in a hairy pile and looked plaintively out of the mesh. I could feel the condemnation in her large, sad eyes.

It took her three days to make her mark. I was walking to the orang house chatting to Liz when I noticed the large, jagged crack in the bullet-proof window.

"Blimey, what's happened here?" Liz mused.

I knew straightaway.

"That's Amy," I said. "Making herself feel at home."

Sure enough, she was sitting in her bed, a look of blissful innocence painted on her impassive features.

"You are a very naughty girl," I told her.

If she could have, I am sure she would have laughed.

Jim had bought the windows from Robin Dunham at Chessington when they knocked down their old ape house. As ever, Jim had driven a hard bargain and, fittingly, he had got them at a knock-down rate. However, the difference between here and there was that the apes at Chessington had just a barren, concrete enclosure. Here, we had tried to make it as interesting as possible and so the first thing Amy had done was find a pebble and hit the window. "Oh that's good, but it doesn't work," she would have told herself. Then she went outside to get a bigger stone. Finally, she had dug a hole and found a great big rock that she had gleefully bashed against the window. "Ah, just the job."

"She's a clever thing, isn't she?" Liz muttered as we

replaced the window with some triple-glazed roofing material.

"Too clever by half," I replied.

Some people will talk of intelligence when it comes to things like this. I don't agree with this because the way people think of intelligence is to compare everything with us humans. That is how we rate intelligence. Orangs are, by nature, very mechanically minded and will use tools. They can work anything out if you give them time. A dog, meanwhile, might round up sheep. A goldfish will not mend your car or round up sheep, but intelligence to me is success in your own environment and there is no need for a goldfish to do either of those things. A goldfish might think, "What the hell do I want to know about brain surgery for? It won't help me in this bowl." I think the analysis of animal intelligence is often an excuse to fly around the world on a grant in the pursuit of letters after your name. Amy had worked out how to break the window of her home. Did that make her intelligent? It certainly made her a nuisance.

A few days later, Amy was to be introduced to another orang-utan. On loan from Chester Zoo, Banghi was 15 days younger and shared his birthday with me. He arrived in a crate in the back of a small van and was accompanied by two care staff. I had prepared his quarters for that first night, separate from Amy's, as I thought that meeting her would be too much after a long road trip, and he spent his first half-hour in his new home trashing his bedroom. He was literally a snotty-nosed youngster. The care staff stayed over for the night to make sure he calmed down and, sure enough, having done his best to dismantle everything, he did. However, I noted that mucus was still running from his nose. I decided to keep an eye on it, but thought he was merely suffering from a cold and fully expected it to go away soon.

The next morning was going to be a momentous one for Amy and me. I thought back to the days at Gordon Mills's estate and then after the accident, when together we had fought for our lives and she had helped me through my darkest times. I pictured her clinging to my shoulders as I cycled to the corner shop and the startled looks on the faces of passers-by. She had stayed with me while her parents had been shipped off to San Diego and had remained as a beacon of light amid all those empty cages filled with nothing but mould and memories. At Chessington I had taken her to see the other orang-utans, just so she knew what they looked like, but did it dawn on her that she was one of them?

I don't honestly know, but I imagine that as far as she was concerned, she was the daughter of this hairy nutter with the scarred head.

So I introduced the pair with more than a little anxiety. But it was a great relief to me that her hand-rearing and totally humanised existence had not had a negative impact on her. Amy eyed him up, started shouting and hollering and gave him a few slaps and thumps. Banghi seemed confused by this show of aggression and tried his best to ignore the abuse directed at him. He turned his back and, before long, Amy got bored. She sat down and looked at this impostor and then got on with her daily business of not doing much.

The following day, after a trouble-free night, I decided to let the two room-mates outside. Amy had evidently been relishing this prospect, as the first thing she did was introduce Banghi to the electric fence. Her unique way of doing this was by pushing him head first into it. Next she decided to give him a lesson on gravity by climbing to the highest part of the climbing apparatus and merrily pushing him off. By now, a somewhat battered Banghi was well aware of their respective roles. Once that was established, the pair settled down to a harmonious life together. Banghi was a good boy and a simple soul and Amy wasn't. They complemented each other perfectly. Thereafter, they loved each other.

11

On the Beach

THE STORM WAS brutal and thundered a destructive path through the park. Branches fell, tiles were shed and the puppet tent was ripped off its hoardings and almost blown away into the grey sky. It felt like the wind of change.

We had survived a second year but that was all. One trait Jim shared with my father was his anxiety about the number of people coming through the gates. At the end of every day, Father used to go to the kiosk by the entrance and ask how many adult tickets had been sold, and Jim was the same, and would forever ring me up from remote parts of the world and ask whether the park was busy. Back then it could not be termed busy by even the most creative imagination. We were clinging to the precipice, holding the pipe dream together with sweaty hands and spare change. And in September 1989 things took a very serious turn for the worse.

The storm had finally blown itself out and I was in the chimp house, measuring up for a new bedroom, when Cindy, the dominant female, took a shine to my tape measure. She bounded over and then, quick as a flash, tore it out of my hand.

"Hey, you!" I shouted. "That's mine! Now give it back!"

Cindy was enjoying her moment of triumph too much to take much notice of me and began examining her new spoils. That was when I crept up to her, leant over and grabbed the tape measure.

"Ha ha, that will teach you," I rejoiced, before the pain kicked in and I saw the blood. "Oh God!" I mused and dropped the tape. Cindy, bemused by this turn-around in events, scooped up the tape measure and sloped off to a safer distance.

I had a nasty gash at the base of my little finger. I was wandering back to the shack to get some first aid, when I came across Jim.

"What's up?" he asked, noting my grimace and the red fist curled around the bleeding finger.

"That Cindy is what's up," I replied bitterly. "She stole my tape measure and I've cut my hand on it."

Jim had a look at my hand and frowned.

"You need to see the doctor with that."

"It will be all right."

Jim fixed me with one of his glares.

"I'm telling you to go to the doctor's," he said. "No argument."

I went to the surgery in nearby Wool and had it stitched up. It seemed fine and the doctor predicted that I would live. I drove back and picked up a spare tape measure from my room. Then I went back to the chimp house to finish the job, making sure Cindy was not in the room at the same time.

I had barely finished the job of dividing the two bedrooms into five when the next problem occurred. I have already remarked that, while Jim had manifold talents, manual labour was not one of them. Hence, with my background in welding and cars and general maintenance, I combined my duties caring for the animals with other roles as architect, builder, plumber, carpenter, janitor and all-round dogsbody. That was why I was manhandling a large propane cylinder around the park and my already weak back gave up. I had struggled with it ever since I had first hurt it while trying to move the carcass of Harry the Bastard, but this was even worse. The pain was excruciating. I somehow struggled on, but the next morning, when I tried to get out of bed, I found I couldn't move. I felt a searing pain whenever I tried to lift myself up.

Worried about what would happen to the animals in my absence, I did not want to make the increasingly familiar trek to hospital, but I came to realise I had no choice. When I got there, things looked even gloomier. I had a general anaesthetic and was put in traction. The days ticked by and I was forced to stay in the hospital in Weymouth with my mood rapidly worsening.

"What's happening with the animals?" I asked Liz.

"I'll cope," she said.

"Look in my address book," I said through gritted teeth. "Find Sean Lord. He might be able to help."

Sean was a good animal man and I knew that he was between jobs. Sure enough, he came to the rescue and helped Liz while I was laid up in bed, anxious and frustrated.

Two weeks passed and I lost two stones in weight before the decision was made to fuse vertebrae together. That was the final straw for me. I was fed up with the dithering and the delays, and did not relish the prospect of a major operation. And so I devised an escape plan. That night, when Liz and Meryl arrived, I told them my idea. They were hesitant but knew there was little point in trying to dissuade me. When the coast was clear, they lifted me up and shuffled me to the edge of the bed. Then, using them as crutches, I hauled myself to my feet and we made our clumsy exit to the car park, where I was shoved in the back of the waiting car. Two days later, I was able to see the chaps again.

Liz made me go to see her chiropractor friend, who examined me and came to a radically different conclusion to the hospital. This new expert said my issue was not my back at all, but the fact that my hips were hopelessly askew. He went to work with his demon fingers and, after much pulling and wrenching, peppered with the occasional shout and swear word, I was sorted.

That was when things became complicated. My injured finger had not healed and would not bend at all. I returned to the doctor in Wool, who admitted that he had not checked for tendon damage, which was a shame because I had severed one. I was referred to a plastic surgery unit at a hospital in Salisbury, where I was given two options. One was a tendon graft, but that would entail a lot of intensive physiotherapy. The second was an arthrodesis operation, which would fuse the finger so it didn't stick out. I came up with a third option and asked whether they could amputate one of the bones. That way the problem would be solved and I could still play the guitar.

They were aghast.

"Oh no," the surgeon huffed. "We only amputate as a last resort."

"Oh well, I suppose we'd better go for the arthrodesis, then."

I managed to secure an afternoon slot for my operation. The procedure required an overnight stay, but that did not fit in with my work routine, so I called on Liz and Meryl to spring me from prison a second time.

Alas, the operation was a disaster. I remember lying on the gurney and listening to the doctor, an Eastern European lady, fretting about where she was going to sleep that night. She had just stepped off the plane and seemed very flustered. I cannot say she filled me with confidence and my fear proved well founded. My finger was left bent outwards and the consultant surgeon now took over and said the only way to rectify it would be to amputate after all, only this time they would have to lose two bones, not the one I had suggested. Thus, I was left with a stump that is good for nothing apart from fretting the sixth guitar string. Nevertheless, I took encouragement from one of my great heroes, the jazz guitarist Django Reinhardt, who had risen to fame after his fingers were badly burnt in a fire at a gypsy camp. I, too, would play the guitar again and was in and out in an hour, later removing my stitches and vowing never again to seek help from doctors. There and then I decided that the NHS could provide me with vaccinations and a death certificate, but otherwise they were to leave me alone.

I was beginning to think that things couldn't get any worse when they actually hit their nadir. Megan, my tiny daughter, was suffering with an ear infection, but it refused to go away and then, to our horror, it developed into a full-blown febrile convulsion. She fitted and was left unconscious. It was incredibly frightening to see a small baby so helpless and we feared the worst. In those circumstances, the pact I had made regarding the NHS was quickly dismissed and I was more than happy to make a quick return to hospital. Thankfully, Megan received expert attention this time and was given a course of antibiotics. Miraculously, she made a complete recovery and my view of the NHS was altered. They had lost one of my fingers but saved my daughter.

With such an extended family, and one that was growing all the time as Jim developed his links with labs and the Templers, I was always at my wits' end. Paddy managed to ensure this remained the case when he developed a problem with a nostril, which was flayed and swollen. I called Ken Pack and he examined him.

"You'll never believe this," he said, shaking his head ruefully.

"What?"

"Well, he's stuck a pebble up his nose," Ken laughed. "That's what's causing the problem."

"Can you get it out?"

Ken had another look.

"It's wedged right up there. I think the best thing to do is leave it. I'm sure it will dislodge itself."

Of course, it didn't do anything of the sort. Nothing is easy with animals, so it wasn't long before Paddy was having a general anaesthetic and we were removing the pebble surgically.

We now had 80 primates. I was in charge of them all, with great help from Liz. However, Liz was juggling her duties with day release at college, so the workload was huge and my days were long and hard. Two nights a week I also drove over to Chippenham, in Wiltshire, to collect bananas from a fruit importer. They wanted me there at 11pm to make the pick-up, but that suited me fine as I'd have been far too busy to get there any earlier. Even with our modest funds we had no option but to seek help and so we took on another member of staff, Julie, to ease the pressure.

Liz and I got back to our building work later in 1989. Our second consignment of chimps was due to arrive from the Templers' Spanish sanctuary and we needed to complete the second temporary structure beforehand. So Liz and I laid a concrete base and built an insulated plywood house. Like many things over the years, it was meant to last only a short time but remained for years.

The chimps arrived on September 5 and the group contained several characters who would become part of Monkey World folklore. Two of them were Charlie and Butch. They arrived in their crates and there was a frenzy of activity. Once again, Jane Goodall put in an appearance. I understood that her presence was good for us, but if the filming and media side of things got in the way of our purpose, I would be less than patient. On such occasions Amy and I were the king and queen of the forest, the grumpy old couple. My diary for that night included the entry: "I reared up in the end to put a stop to the circus." One can only push me so far.

Charlie was in a terrible condition. The Templers had done all they could for him, but he had suffered horrifically beforehand and was a malnourished, underweight, ragtail chimp with a lopsided jaw and a mesh of scars on his body. Yet from the start there was something special about him, and Jim, in particular, bonded with him. It was hard to imagine back then that two decades on, a magnificent bronze bust of Jim and Charlie would sit in the park, a tribute to their friendship and two resolute personalities.

We never really knew how old Charlie was. All we did know was that he had been used as a money-earner by a beach photographer and had endured a horrible life. His owner had beaten him repeatedly with a machete and his jaw had been mangled by the ferocious blows. In fact, his jaw was so badly broken that there was no room for incisors in his jagged, lopsided mouth.

A chimp's weapons are strength and teeth, so these photographers would sometimes crush their spirit with repeated beatings and even remove their teeth. We saw one of the worst examples of this treatment much later when poor old Bryan arrived. He had been smuggled from Africa, through Cuba and into Mexico, where a photographer kept him in a box by the side of the road and smashed his teeth out with a hammer. Shards of teeth were driven deep up into his gums and I suspect he had other teeth removed with pliers. Now Bryan has a good quality of life, but sometimes I will see him sitting in the corner of his enclosure, gently rocking as he remembers the sheer hell of those years.

To add to Charlie's list of problems, he had also been given drugs. This happened with many chimps. Owners would inject their animals with diazepam, more commonly known as Valium, to control them. In those days you could buy the sedative from the corner chemist in Spain. So they did. It was another way of making the chimps do as they were told. Many became addicted.

Understandably, Charlie had issues and I grimaced when I looked at the criss-cross pattern of blackened lines on his head. We housed the new arrivals and I watched them settle into their new surroundings. The sun was setting when suddenly I heard a huge commotion. I rushed to the chimps' enclosure.

"What is it?" I yelled to no one in particular.

That was when I saw Charlie beating his chest and screaming towards the perimeter fence and the passing road. I looked over and heard the slow, familiar rumble of a tank passing on its way to the neighbouring Bovington camp. Charlie was absorbed by this scene. He stood at the highest point he could find and roared. Displaying is generally a good thing for chimps, but in this instance it was also slightly sad and reminded me of Don Quixote tilting at windmills. Charlie the chimp was tilting at tanks. I am sorry to say that Charlie had mental health issues. He was a sweetheart and you could do what you wanted with him, but the sad reason behind this malleable and compliant personality was that he had been brutally conditioned to be that way. Whatever the issues and the history, however, Charlie soon settled down to being one of our most beloved chimps.

Butch was different. He was younger and the beach photographer had handed him over because he could no longer cope with him. Sometimes it was like that. The photographers were just happy to get rid of them and didn't go to the sordid lengths of attacking them with tools or turning them into drug addicts. Butch was a dominant animal and would go on to be the kingpin in the bachelor group. You don't reach such heights unless you are a bit rufty tufty and Butch certainly was. It also meant he could be tougher to deal with, whereas Charlie was the most forgiving soul. Maybe that was down to the fact that, if you've been beaten to within an inch of your life, you just get on with things.

I always found it fascinating watching how these individuals asserted themselves within a group and how the hierarchy of the group was formed. Broadly speaking, a chimp group functions in a similar way to a human one. If I'm bigger and more powerful than you, we'll do it my way. Then, in turn, you may do things sneakily behind my back. I imagine this way of operating is the same from the chimp house to global corporations.

The female ape hierarchy is exactly the same as that of humans too – absolutely nobody understands it! The behaviour of the female ape is directly related to menstrual cycles. Do they get PMT? Oh my goodness, yes! When she is menstruating, the female chimp's bottom blows up like a football. We ended up putting all our chimps on the pill, and the peace and harmony that ensued was a blissful bonus. The main reason for using contraception, though, was the fact that we were a rescue centre. Every baby that was born on site meant there was one less place for an abused or neglected animal. We have never lost sight of that ideal.

Charlie rapidly became a favourite of mine too. Others never quite reached that billing. You have people you prefer and it is the same with animals. One chimp who I was less enamoured of was Taffy, a contrary chap who would always do the polar opposite to what you wanted.

It was Christmas 1989 and the sun broke over the snowy trails. We had got through another year and the park had grown. It felt like a family affair. Jamie was helping Albert take money for the go-karts and, in time, Megan would start working in the café. There was much to celebrate, but looking after scores of primates is a never-ending task. As I blew cold steam into the frozen air, I could feel my blood rising. As usual, Taffy was refusing to do what I wanted. I knew he had a cold, but he was always an awkward so-and-so and, on occasion, could be quite spiteful.

"Come on, Taffy, give me a break," I muttered as he refused to leave his quarters so I could clean them. Things carried on in this vein for a while, with neither of us going anywhere.

"Oh for God's sake!" I cried. "Why don't you just drop dead?"

Two days later he did. The cold turned to a respiratory infection and then to pneumonia. It was the day

1. I use Bertha the leopard tortoise for a footstool, back in the days of Pan's Garden, circa 1960.

2 & 3. Dear Horace at Little Rhondda during my spell as the rock ' n' roll zookeeper in 1976

4. Harry the Bastard

5. Introducing Jamie to Katie in the summer of '77

Two young animals who failed to make it – Rimba, born at Little Rhondda (6, top) and Simone, Monkey World's first chimp birth (7, bottom).

8 & 9. The cantankerous Amy in her infant days.

Part of the family. Amy gets creative with Jamie (10, top)
and is introduced to a wary looking Kenyon
at Monkey World (11, bottom)

12. Amy in her clingy days.

13. Apes on a plane – me and RoRo on our way back from the Pingtung Rescue Centre in Taiwan.

14. With Jim and Charlie, two dearly-departed friends now immortalised by a statue in Monkey World

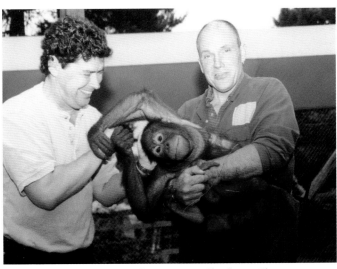

15. Gordon forces a smile from Jim

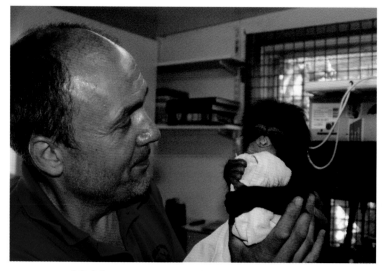

16. They grow up so fast. With Rodders.

17. Arfur, the capuchin, eavesdrops on a conversation

18. Amy in one of her gentler moods with Gordon. Alison is to the right. Note the scar on my head, a relic of the car crash.

19. Johni performs for Jim, Alison and me

20. I've always got my hands full at Monkey World. This time it's Eveline and Seamus as Jim snaps away.

21. With my fifth and best wife Lou after our wedding in St Lucia, 2008

22. Sally and Bryan. I have formed a strong
bond with Sally who has become Monkey
World's top class foster mum.

23. Jess and Arfur

24. With my daughter, Megan

25. I have always had a sense of wanderlust.
Here I introduce my grandson Josh to it.

26. This is A-mei, our resident urang-utan foster mum

27. Sally and I share a tender moment.

28. Uneasy rider.
It's been
quite a journey.

before Christmas Eve. Everyone was in good spirits and trying to summon up some goodwill. I felt terrible, a Scrooge-like ogre who had wished ill on poor Taffy. The guilt was huge.

Taffy was the first chimp we had lost at Monkey World and that, combined with my cruel words, left me succumbing to a welter of emotions. I walked past Amy. She looked at me through the fence. I couldn't say anything, but realised how privileged I was to share the lives of these wonderful creatures, however awkward they could be. I hurried back to my shack in a daze and fired up my Suzuki GS550 motorbike. I didn't know where I was going, but I needed to escape, so I hit the open road, taking my emotions out on the frosted tarmac and shimmering hills.

I headed towards Bridport, as the roads were quiet out there and the dips exhilarating. The speed focused my mind and meant, fleetingly, I could not dwell on Taffy's fate. I leant into the bends and opened the throttle. Then, riding over the downs, I suffered a front-end blow-out. Pulses of panic surged through my brain. In a nanosecond I pictured by friend and fellow biker, Robin Dunham, telling me one day that it was impossible to suffer a front puncture at more than 30mph and not have a major crash.

I had no idea how fast I was going but I knew it was much, much faster than that. I was a moment from disaster. But then, suddenly and unexpectedly, I realised the bike had not slid into the fence or hit the wall of trees. Somehow, it had stayed upright and stuttered to a slow stop by the side of the road. My knuckles were white as I took them off the handlebars. It was a little miracle.

I parked the bike up a muddy lane and started walking. I was not sure where I was going, but I had an urge to keep moving. I could hear the sea off to my left and so I headed for that. It was, by now, the dead of night, and the air was black and blue with cold. I traipsed onto the beach and listened to the crunch of pebbles beneath my feet. I sat down and looked out to the waves lined with white spray. I picked up a pebble and then another, noting how it was amazing that they all seemed to be exactly the same size. I began drifting into reveries about life and death. About why some of us are saved and others die.

That was when I realised where I was.

"Blimey," I said. "That's fitting."

I was on West Bay beach, the same place where Reggie Perrin had faked his suicide in the TV sitcom. I thought briefly about whether I should do a Reggie and just disappear.

I should mention that, ever since my car crash, I struggle to recall my dreams. I don't mind because my fantasy world is very important to me and I don't need to be asleep to get there. It's where I can escape without a motorbike. I sat on the beach and departed reality for a few minutes. It was a release from the cruelty of the natural world. Then I started talking to myself, another trait, and began pulling myself together.

"Come on, Keeling," I whispered.

"Get a grip on it, you idiot," I replied.

"Well, what do you want to do? Sit here thinking about the meaning of life all night or get on with your life?"

I opted for the latter. I thumbed a lift most of the way home and then returned with the Monkey World van to pick up my stricken Suzuki. By the time I got to bed, I was mentally and physically exhausted, but I was up in time to see to the chaps the next morning. My midnight flit remained a secret. Taffy was buried on the site. Life went on.

12

Freefall

CHATTA ARRIVED THE following November. She was yet another chimp who had been used in the beach photography trade in Spain and had been rescued by the Templers. She needed a home and, even though we were struggling to keep afloat and money was always stretched beyond the limit, we were never ones to turn down the needy if we had room.

As she was very young and weighed less than 10 kilos, it was unthinkable to put her in with any of the existing chimp groups. So I volunteered a room in my ramshackle bungalow to accommodate the latest orphan for at least the six-month quarantine period.

How nice, I am sure you are thinking. How wrong. Whereas I had toiled with Amy and shared many ups and downs, we had always got on in our own unique way. There had been some sort of bond from the start. But Chatta was an extremely hardened individual with very little to give socially. They were traits that would have served her well as she tried to cope with her pitiful life as a photographer's prop, but they made for frustrating times at Chateau Keeling.

Independent and very clever, Chatta needed no affection or physical contact, but she made it very clear what she did want. "I want food, toys and the best seat," she would say without speaking the words. "And I want them now."

Nevertheless, Chatta and I developed a passable working relationship and, once the quarantine period was over, she moved into the park to live with her own species, finding her place as a low-ranking female. She got on with everyone, which goes to show that animals are designed to live with their own kind.

Jim was also working tirelessly during this time. More and more monkeys were arriving from various laboratories, but Jim was also spending a lot of time outside of the park. One of his key interests was diet and he was developing a pellet food that would be suitable for primates. Although one already existed in the UK, we wanted a product that was more palatable to the poor souls who were going to have to eat the stuff. I offered Jim the data I had collected from my time in San Diego and he burnt the midnight oil in search of a better solution. He also took a TV presenting role that meant he needed to drive to Birmingham on a regular basis. Added to the day-to-day dramas and the over-riding goal of saving abused and neglected primates, it was clear that Jim's plate was full to overflowing.

I realised just how much during the winter of 1990. Jim had returned to New York as usual to spend the festive season with his family. Meanwhile, I got a call from my bank and was told my pay cheque had bounced. I rang Jim.

"Is everything all right?" I asked.

"Yes, yes," he said. "Just cash flow. I'll sort it out."

Being an honourable man, Jim did sort it out and it never happened again. But it made me realise just how close to the wind we were sailing.

While Jim was in New York, I also realised that matters were coming to a head with Steve Matthews, one of his partners. Both were ambitious and liked control. I sensed that the situation could not carry on. To cap it all, it was also well known among the staff that Jim's marriage was now in an irreparable state. The crunch was coming.

I have seen few people cope with a crisis quite like Jim Cronin. With his back against the wall, he came into his own. He was like a caged animal and when pushed into a corner, he extended his claws and flexed his muscles. Day-to-day routines and humdrum maintenance rendered Jim a useless and annoying hindrance, but under pressure he was unparalleled in his tenacity and abilities. And so on March 8, 1991, Jim became the sole owner of Monkey World, negotiating a new lease with our landlord that enabled him to buy the park. We were out of trouble. For the moment.

Jim also approved plans to replace my corrugated-iron shack, the makeshift home I had moved into for what I'd been told was "a maximum of six months" some four years earlier. True to his word, an excellent bungalow was quickly built with the aid of a new-found cash injection.

We also gained a new ally in the form of John Lewis, a veterinary surgeon extraordinaire. A partner in International Zoo Veterinary Group, John was a huge asset. On his first day helping us, he performed anaesthesia on all of our chimpanzees for general health checks. He also looked at Banghi, Amy's by now beloved partner.

Banghi's snotty nose had not cleared up in the intervening years and, with John's input, the full scale of his problems was laid bare. One of the issues was with his throat sac. The orang uses his sac to make his distinctive long-distance call. The sound resonates inside and echoes. It is basically a dead area, with very poor blood flow, and so any infection within it can be very hard to shift. Banghi had a problem and would undergo numerous operations in the ensuing years in an attempt to resolve it. The throat sac was opened up and washed out with peroxide. Then John made holes in the sac so that fluid could drain away. Banghi was also given very potent antibiotics at one stage, which had to be administered by injection every six hours. That meant I would get up at 4am so that he could be darted. It was a tortuous path with him but we did everything we could. Still, though, he struggled to shake off his problems.

A boost to business came via an unlikely source. Anneka Rice was a TV celebrity who was fronting a programme in which she had to complete some task within a certain time frame. The very popular programme was called *Challenge Anneka* and I have to confess I knew nothing about it. However, I did later hear that one task, in which they were supposed to revamp the famous White Horse landmark in Dorset, was likened to a bit of do-it-yourself landscape gardening.

Nevertheless, we agreed that they could help us build accommodation for six chimps arriving from Spain. To make the challenge seem even less likely to succeed, the project would involve constructing not one, but two identical houses. Perhaps I am being cynical, but I believe they took on impossible tasks every so often just to maintain the suspense and drama throughout the rest of the series, and I wonder now whether we were one of those. I found the whole experience a bit of a con. The only person who really didn't know what the challenge was going to be was Anneka, because all the tradesmen involved would be sitting in their truck, parked up the road, waiting for the call.

It soon became clear that the task was not going to succeed. As I have stated, I am a grumpy old man, so it was all too much for me. I thought, if they really wanted to help then why set an arbitrary time limit? So with time running out, we decided we should focus all our efforts on getting one house ready for the chaps.

The trucks arrived. A quarantine official was already on site, which was highly unusual too, ready to put his seal of approval on the finished structure. In a nail-biting, made-for-TV finale, the last nails were banged in just in time. And so we were able to release Chico, Mojo, Rocky, Peggy, Kylo and Mona.

Poor old Mona was in a sorry state. She had been kept in a tiny box and fed a terrible diet of gruel for her whole life. Consequently, she was a stunted, crooked figure. It was awful to watch her and I felt a little resentful of the glare of the TV cameras. As soon as they stopped rolling, the crew departed and the workmen followed. It was amazing to see how quickly they vacated the place, leaving the job clearly unfinished. The whole affair left a somewhat bitter taste in the mouth, because this was not a game.

I introduced Chatta to the group and, after an awful lot of initial excitement, she settled down to a life with her own species, but it would be some considerable time before we could afford to complete that second house.

That October our first chimp birth was recorded. The mother was Clin, a hard-case chimp named after my father and hailing from the Congo, with the heavy eyebrows and lanky body characteristic of the region. She had been rescued from a French lab, was blind in one eye and had the number 552 tattooed on the inside of her thigh. She was an indomitable figure and you did not want to get on the wrong side of her. Clin did shows signs of wanting to care for Simone, but five days after the birth it was clear that the infant was not thriving and would need to be bottle-reared if she was to have a chance.

Once again I found myself sharing my home with a tiny animal, handing out bottle feeds every two hours, 24 hours a day. Jamie was now 16 and he lent a hand, which was much appreciated as I was devoting a lot of time to finishing the Anneka challenge. We also had two new staff members. After several unsuitable candidates came and went, Liz found two lads, Matt and Christian, who proved responsible, decent folk.

I became increasingly friendly with John Lewis as we spent more and more time with each other. In the ensuing months we fought a two-pronged battle, trying to protect Simone from the numerous ailments that her weak body was struggling to resist, and desperately trying to make headway with Banghi. Promising days were followed by ones of utmost despair as we struggled to keep these two alive. By early April, Simone had declined to a barely conscious state. Racking his brains for a solution, Jim even approached the local hospital where, with his gift of the gab, he managed to enlist the help of a paediatrician. John also worked around the clock to monitor Simone's condition. It was no use. At 9pm on April 11, 1992, Simone gave up her struggle and succumbed. I will never become accustomed to losing an animal and it is something I can never accept without some difficulty. It may be nature but that does not make it any easier.

I buried myself in my work: building bedrooms for the surviving chimps in the old Anneka Rice homes, now rechristened the Templer Pavilions in honour of Simon and Peggy; servicing the generator that powered the café; and welding the chassis of the ancient van that was facing its own MOT d-day. And there was still Banghi, gamely battling on against his own ailing health and refusing to submit to his regular bouts of pneumonia.

The park was growing and there was always a new mouth to feed. In this ever-changing world I was glad to take solace in Amy's peculiar company. Oh, she could still be the crusty old girl that she had always been, and she often drove me to distraction, but she was a constant and a reminder of where we had all come from.

I got out of the park for a rare excursion to do a parachute jump alongside a young, blind lady named Tina Pryke, in an effort to raise funds for the park.

Meryl, meanwhile, went on a scuba-diving trip that weekend. As my plane climbed through the clouds, it never occurred to me that our differing excursions were strangely symbolic of the gulf that had grown between us. Liz chaperoned Megan and Kenyon as the plane reached the designated height of 13,000 feet. The nerves were rampant and the sight stunning. There was no turning back. Not with so much at stake for the park. The door was pulled open, our harnesses were checked and the pilot gave the thumbs up. Tina and I stood briefly on the threshold and I half wished I couldn't see the mindboggling drop in front of us either. Then we were out and plummeting. Those few minutes of ear-splitting freefall, followed by the tranquillity of floating to earth, were a breathtaking experience. As soon as I landed I wanted to do it again.

I felt pleased as I headed back to the park, knowing Tina and I had raised a considerable sum of money and still thrilling at the memory of our descent. It was late, the last calls of the apes had dwindled and the park took on that twilight slump of satisfaction. Then Meryl arrived back from Cornwall.

"I haven't missed any of you at all," she said accusingly as soon as she made it through the door. Then she turned to me. "And I'm leaving you."

Jim and I were now bonded by our broken marriages as well as our daily pipe dream-cum-nightmare. It was hard for me to wave goodbye to Megan and Kenyon, who went with their mother. Of course, I still saw them a lot, and they loved returning to see the animals they had grown up with, but it was not the same. However, I did not burden Jim with my personal problems, nor him me. A grunt here or there and a knowing look was the only acknowledgement of our parallel suffering.

I coped with the situation by burying my head in the sand and throwing myself even deeper into the care and well-being of my other family. And I always had Amy, not much of a looker I admit, but a reliable presence all the same. You couldn't say she was moody because she was constantly in a bad one.

Jim, on the other hand, never suited a life alone. He was a sociable figure devoid of domestic abilities. In those months, his health suffered terribly, both physically and mentally. He entered a fug of depression and I grew slightly alarmed by his self-neglect. That November I was clearing out one of the enclosures when word got to me that Jim had collapsed. It had all added up. The poor lifestyle, the failed marriage, the trickle of visitors and the stress and strain that came from spiralling interest rates. The future had never looked so bleak.

13

Births, Deaths, Marriages

I TRY TO be pragmatic and do not show my emotions, but it was with a paternal sense of satisfaction that I noticed the tell-tale, grape-like swellings around Amy's rear end.

"You're pregnant, old girl," I told her as the hairball shuffled around her enclosure one morning. "Congratulations."

Banghi had evidently forgiven her for pushing him into the electric fence on his first morning at Monkey World.

It was welcome news. I was thrilled at the thought of breeding orangs and the fact that Amy was the mother-to-be only made it more special. I felt a surge of satisfaction at having struggled through those perilous first three months of life, relentlessly feeding her and imploring her to keep on fighting. I felt a flash of gratitude for us both managing to escape from the mangled wreckage by the M2 without everlasting injuries. Well, apart from my brain damage.

This being Monkey World, problems still abounded, as Liz found to her cost. Butch was now established as the chief thug of the hooligan group. I liked him but he was a handful and he certainly took no prisoners. One day Liz was operating a steel sliding door in the chimp enclosure. Butch had noted her efforts and, for a lark, leapt into range and ripped the door from her grasp. The door slammed into Liz's arm. She was trapped and roared out in pain.

"Oh God, what now?" I mumbled as I ran from the other side of the enclosure to where Liz was impaled, while Butch voiced his approval. I released the door and Liz collapsed to the floor in agony.

"I think it's broken," she cried.

I took her to Poole Hospital where they confirmed she had a badly broken limb. I felt terrible for Liz and almost as bad for myself, as it would be hard to keep the park ticking over without her invaluable input. One of the problems with animal husbandry is that, despite the joy of working with some wonderful beasts, the fact is it is an anti-social job that pays a pittance. The concept of working seven days a week for next to nothing generally only appeals to committed eccentrics, so there is a high turnover of staff. The following year we would lose Matt and Christian, and the temporary loss of Liz cut a slashing wound.

To lower my spirits even further, my son Jamie turned 17 and decided to leave home. I was happy for him to go off and make a life for himself, as I was with all three kids, but it was still a wrench. Now I was on my own again, with only my furballs for company. Meanwhile, Jim's health slowly recovered. He was still not himself but, like me, he felt the best therapy was to throw himself back into his work. We were still attracting far too few guests for commercial comfort, but we continued to accept new primate rescues with unabated enthusiasm.

"That's our mission," Jim barked if anyone questioned the financial wisdom of what he was doing. "We're not in this to make money. We're doing it for the animals."

He would always abide by one enduring principle too, which was never to pay for any animal. Ethics, I am glad to say, had changed since the 1970s.

And so, when Windsor Safari Park closed, Jim was quickly on the telephone and entered into negotiations with the official receivers. I knew he would get his way and, sure enough, we agreed to rehome the chimpanzee group comprising Rodney, Buxom, Jestah, Jane, Jess, Bixa and Evie.

They were a nice group. Several years later I would try an audacious introduction of all of Paddy's group to Rodney's group. It was a bit like the chimp version of *West Side Story*. With chimps, there is always one dominant male and so this situation quickly became a showdown between Paddy and Rodney. I felt instinctively that, despite popular wisdom, they would be able to co-exist; you cannot make one person like another, but you can also wind them up to the point of hysteria by only letting them see each other every day through a fence.

It was a calculated risk, but I knew I would be able to separate them before things got too out of hand. Inevitably, there was a lot of shouting and bawling, posturing and politics, but in a short space of time I completed the introduction around the central pavilion.

"Serious amount of vocals," I wrote in my diary that

night. "Both Paddy and Cindy got superficial cuts, red welts on their backs, but otherwise blood-free. Gave them all access to all three pavilions and bedrooms."

It was a huge success.

But back then, when Rodney's group first arrived, they had their own quarters. Jim bought me a welding mask and I set about extending the Templer Pavilion to accommodate the new guests. It should be said I was always a very cheap welder.

We had a number of chimp births, which was a problem as allowing our apes to breed in an uncontrolled manner could soon lead to issues of overpopulation. It was important that we never lost sight of the fact that we were – and are – primarily a rescue centre for individuals. We would like to take more animals than we do, but sometimes we just have to say no. Hence, breeding is also an issue. We do allow a certain amount of controlled breeding, such as with the woolly monkeys and orangs, or for the well-being of a certain group, but our fundamental role is to rescue animals.

So the periodic births presented a problem and the answer was to put some of our females on the pill, hidden in a small amount of fruit juice. But there were accidents and a few babies arrived. Some chimps, like

Sally, were fine with the pill. Others weren't, like Lulu, who would keep it in her mouth and then, when you weren't looking, spit it out.

So we spoke to John Lewis and he suggested we start using contraceptive implants. It was a radical idea which involved putting an implant, the size of a small Biro refill, on a hypodermic needle and injecting it under the skin. It worked for a while, but then the chimps started pulling them out. They would groom each other, find a lump and think, "What's this?" Then they would dig in their fingers and remove the implant.

We also started clicker training to help with giving our apes their jabs. This is a simple method of communication that involves a series of hand signals. If the ape does what you want it to do, you give it a click with the clicker. Personally, I think it is a bit of a con, and if an ape is doing what you ask, a click is a pretty measly reward. Therefore, I tend to give them something more, like a nice drink or a sweet. Fair's fair.

It takes two or three months for a chimp to learn the signs if you repeat them every day. You can use this method with all apes, although God bless the gibbons, there is not a lot going on up there. It means if I make a certain signal, the animal will present its mouth or ear for examination. Most importantly, it will offer its shoulder, which is very useful, because it means we can inject it in the deltoid muscle, where there are no major veins or nerves and so little scope for anything to go wrong. By contrast, if you dart an animal, it is more stressful for it and you can also miss or get the wrong bit. Nobody wants a dart in their eye. It is my firm belief that clicker training serves a useful purpose, although we might be better served using it on humans.

It was ironic that, while we were trying to prevent chimp pregnancies, Amy's went wrong. The old girl was pregnant by Banghi and I was keeping my fingers crossed for her, but sadly she had a miscarriage. To make matters worse, Banghi's health was not improving. He had another throat sac operation and we racked our brains for ways of helping him with his respiraratory issues. I would go to the orang house in the dead of night to give him a particularly strong antibiotic known as gentamicin. He took the course and I started crossing my fingers for him instead of Amy.

In my diary for March 1994 I wrote: "I had a few hours off around midday to get married."

My third wife, Janet, was the result of a whirlwind

one-month romance. I can only recall that it seemed like a good idea at the time.

The following year would prove significant for several reasons. In the spring I packed a load of fencing components into a chimpanzee travelling crate, which was sent off to Nigeria. The destination was a primate rescue project called Pandrillus, run by Peter Jenkins and Liza Gadsby. They had started work in Cameroon and Nigeria in 1988 and were now committed to saving the endangered drill monkeys from extinction. The donation showed how Jim's vision had reaped a rich dividend, as we were now considered experts in using electric fences as a form of confinement for primates. We were eager to help Peter and Liza and pleased that others saw the advantage of using this cheap and less intimidating form of restraint.

It was that July when I made my first diary entry about someone who was to change things at Monkey World for ever. Both Jim and I had been through the mill. We had been in hospital and we had balanced the joy of seeing the pipe dream realised with the underlying fear that it might be wrenched away at any time. Money was still an issue and, although Jim kept much of it from me, I knew we were only just about surviving. The thought of the park closing and having to rehome all these wonderful animals, including Amy, now that I had set her free and made her live as an ape, hung over us like a sword.

But then another American arrived at the park and things changed, especially for Jim. Alison Ames, a behavioural expert who had studied biological anthropology at Cambridge University, had visited with a view to discussing fencing techniques. She had been working overseas with bears for another organisation and she and Jim chatted about the whys and wherefores of electric fencing. Clearly, there was a rapport between them and Jim took Alison in with Sally, our remarkably intelligent and relatively safe chimp. Jim gave Sally some paper and crayons and she was more than happy to play along and impress everyone with her artistic sensibility.

It is actually very rare for a chimp not to focus on art as an interesting pastime if given the opportunity. So Sally looked at her work and marvelled at the lines produced by the crayon. Perhaps an eyewitness would have taken it as a true example of just how intelligent chimps are, at least until the point where Sally grew bored and started to eat the crayon.

Sally's role as matchmaker obviously worked as Jim and Alison became constant companions. He may well have been seeing her before then, but Jim always played his cards very close to his chest. It was as if he would have to kill you if he told you anything.

Alison was a very practical person and I quickly realised I would be able to work closely with her. She brought new and interesting ideas to the park at a time of poverty and declining visitor numbers. A small example was when she meekly asked if she could clear a corner of the storeroom to serve as somewhere to do her university studies. In a flash Alison had transformed the gloomy clutter of this dumping ground into a pleasant working environment where our adoption scheme was born. Jim's eyes lit up in admiration and he moved his desk into the same room to be close to his soul-mate.

But this was Monkey World and there was always a trauma lurking around the corner. So as Alison managed to haul Jim out of his depression, I jumped over a tiny fence, enclosing the rabbits in the domestic animals section, and cried out in pain. The tendons had pulled away from the bone in my foot and I couldn't walk an inch. However, ever since I had been bitten by Pablo the chimp and had seen my brother, Pie, mopping up my blood on the kitchen tiles as I turned a whiter shade of pale, I had tried to avoid hospitals. The trouble with my back and finger had only strengthened that belief. On this occasion, I tried to avoid them by having Dave, one of our animal care staff, push me around the park in a wheelbarrow, but it was no use. I soon had no choice but to make the unwanted journey to hospital, where I was put in a plaster cast. The following day I hobbled back to the orang house on my crutches. Amy was ambivalent, but Banghi was hysterical at the sight of this curious-looking foot. God knows quite what was going on in his head, but he refused to come to bed that night for fear of the alien limb.

Not only did the cast look strange, but it was agonising. I dosed myself up with Voltarol, but the pain festered and I went back to the hospital to get a second opinion. Cue a second cast which was more painful than the first. I limped around the park on my crutches, growing increasingly frustrated and irritable, until I decided that enough was enough. I went to the tool shed, got my angle grinder and cut the thing off myself. That was when I cut my fingers. Like I said, trauma was always in the air. You'd need a corner turned but end up with a tourniquet.

The next few years epitomised the rollercoaster experience of life, both for humans and primates. In

1996 Jim and Alison were married and I began to think the park might finally survive. Alison's expertise and practical common sense were perfect for tethering Jim's huge ambition, and the numbers of people coming through the gates slowly increased.

Like Jim, I also found a new partner. It had been a rash decision to marry Janet and we bowed to the inevitable. I began to wonder whether my devotion to a grumpy old ape like Amy had rendered me incompatible with women, but started a relationship with Mel, another employee who joined us on a job creation scheme. It did not take long for a new romance to blossom and it would end up in another marriage. This one might best be described by the saying: "When it was good it was very, very good, but when it was bad it was horrid."

Then Amy fell pregnant again. I clung to the hope that this time might be different, but reality nagged away at me and told me to expect the worst. I had witnessed many births at Monkey World and in my previous lives at Howletts, Little Rhondda and Colchester, but this time was different. Amy was the only animal who actually belonged to me. She could be a world-class misery guts, but we had been in it together, for better or worse, since I had got her through her first year with a borrowed incubator and Evil Edna.

It was winter again. Alison was on her way into the park when she called me on my radio.

"Hello, Jeremy, where are you?" she asked through the crackling.

Little lips flicked the tip of my finger.

"I'm saying hello to Gordon," I replied.

There was a static pause. Then Alison clicked back. "Who's Gordon?"

I had visited Amy late the previous night and all seemed well. My estimates of delivery dates were usually accurate, so I knew it was close. I had already separated Amy and Banghi because it is a grim fact of the natural world that male orangs are often not nice to babies. I said goodnight to both and then returned first thing in the morning to find a bundle of wispy hair shrouding a couple of large brown eyes.

"Good for you, Amy."

Amy had cleaned up Gordon but it was already obvious that she did not know what to do. You can play psychologist and plough for reasons, but I think it is a simple case of nature and nurture. As with humans, if a child is neglected by poor parents, the chances are it will then become a poor parent itself, and Amy's mother, Jane, had never reared a baby and could not get away from her offspring fast enough. When Amy put Gordon down, I took that as the sign. An orang should never do that to a baby, so I realised we would have to take Gordon out.

That was sad. It would have been nice to think that Amy could have formed a happy, contented family group. I also remembered how, despite her absence of mothering skills, I had been told that Jane had actually nursed a baby chimpanzee during her days at Belle Vue Zoo. She had carried it around and cared for it, although it was clearly weaned, and I took solace from that. If Jane, for all her faults, had some carefully hidden maternal instinct, then maybe, deep down, Amy did too.

I went in with Amy and tried to encourage her to fend for Gordon, but she adopted an air of utter indifference. John Lewis was present with a dart gun and sedative, just in case Amy turned nasty. She didn't and I never expected her to, but you cannot be too careful with mothers and children, as I knew from bitter experience. I felt sorry for Amy. I think the poor thing just had no idea what to do. I thought back to my own childhood and my mother's lack of maternal instincts and sympathised.

It was strange to have Gordon in my house that

night. It was 14 years since I had carried out a similar vigil on behalf of his mother. Now I did the same for him. A few days later, I handed Gordon over to Mike Colbourne, my co-keeper, and although I knew it made sense because of my duties elsewhere, it was hard to let go. Because of Amy's involvement, I felt Gordon was special to me and my family.

It was around a year later when Gordon came back. Banghi's health eventually caught up with him. His breathing was so erratic that John took him to our on-site surgery, where he was given an anaesthetic so that he could be checked over. He put his stethoscope to Banghi's chest and listened. John grimaced. It was clear only a tiny percentage of Banghi's lung was working and the poor fella was in distress. I let Jim know the severity of it and he came over. That was when we all agreed that the kindest thing to do was put Banghi to sleep.

I turned my attention to Gordon. The way to reintroduce a young primate is to take it to the ape house each day and put it in special living quarters. That means it is separated from the adults but gets used to seeing them and how they behave. It allowed Gordon to make a connection with Amy, our only adult orang now that Banghi had died, and realise that this place was where he lived. Mike would still take him home each night, but eventually, we decided the time was right, so I went in and sat with Gordon and Amy. Initially, those maternal instincts remained buried deep down and dormant, but I played with Gordon and tried to make conversation.

"Look, Amy, this is Gordon. Say hello."

Amy huffed and did the orang equivalent of a shrug. The next day I put Gordon down next to me on the floor of the orang house. This was the way I had done it before. Put the infant down next to you and casually move a foot away. Then put it two feet away. Finally, you put it down, shut the door and run like hell.

It took some time, but Amy and Gordon gradually grew to love each other. Indeed, before long, Gordon would simply refuse to go anywhere without Amy. They were joined at the hip. Did they know they were mother and son? Who knows? It is such an inexact science, which is what makes it such fun, but it was clear there was some sort of bond between Gordon and this irascible old girl who could sometimes be as friendly as a bad case of haemorrhoids. Amy is a hard animal and Gordon had to dig away at that tough, grizzled exterior to find the soft underbelly of the mother ape. It had been Monkey World's first orang birth. And I was now a surrogate grandmother.

14

The Circus

TRUDY THE CHIMPANZEE became a cause célèbre and a national debate, but to me she was just another animal who needed caring for when she arrived at the park in April 1998. She was in a bad way. It was not that she was particularly frightened of contact but that she went into what can best be described as shutdown mode. She would sit in the window of the nursery and rock gently. The mental scars were evident in her vacant stare. It would be another nine months before her case reached its explosive climax outside Aldershot Magistrates Court.

I never get involved in the political side of the

rescues, leaving that to Jim and Alison and their campaigning fervour, but it was impossible not to get dragged into the emotional maelstrom caused by Trudy. A group known as Animal Defenders had infiltrated the Hampshire farm of Mary Chipperfield, the famous circus trainer, and taken some undercover footage of her trying to get Trudy into a box. It made for harrowing viewing as Chipperfield cried, "I'm not in the mood" and "you can bloody cry" while beating Trudy with some sort of stick in an effort to get her into a dog's travelling box.

The footage led to Chipperfield facing 21 charges of animal cruelty. In addition, her husband, Richard Cawley, faced seven charges. The grainy video also showed an elephant being beaten with a spade and an iron bar. A detective had approached Jim and told him that there was a baby chimp who was likely to become part of a high-profile court case. They wanted to know if Jim would take her should the court case be successful. Jim said no. He wanted Trudy now.

So Trudy arrived and I tried to get her used to her new home. I had seen the video and, in a way, I was not surprised. It's what some people do to get an animal to do something it doesn't want to. Trudy, though, was clearly traumatised and I decided to try her with our nursery group, where Sally was the resident mum and matron.

Sally had arrived from the Templers in 1993 and her case highlighted the intricacies that exist in chimpanzee politics. Among the males, the dominant one is the policeman, both inside the group and out. If something horrible is happening inside the group then he will go and kick arse. If something from outside happens that impacts on the group, he is the first line of defence. But much like with humans, the female's role in the group is far more complex. In a nutshell, though, she will let the bloke think he is in charge and say he is wonderful. That means she can then use his muscle and bravado to do the dirty work. The basic politics of the group is actually sorted out by the dominant females. That's my take, anyway.

Sally went into Paddy's group and she simply could not get her head around the fact that she was not in charge. Her way of coping with this was to scream and scream until she was sick. She was kicked out of the group and condemned to a half-life on the periphery. Orangs are very stoic animals and can cope very well with such a scenario, but a chimp is not conditioned to a solitary life, so Sally needed help. We had an opportunity for her to work with youngsters and I therefore took her out and put her in with the nursery group.

We got on well. So much so that if I happened to go down there with a woman, Sally would fly into a jealous rage and scream that she wanted my companion dead. I quickly realised it was best to visit alone. Although it was the little boys she really loved, Sally would also do her best for the females. Trudy, though, was a challenge even for her.

It was then that Jim delivered his bombshell. Always very concerned about the dos and don'ts of families, Jim collared me one day and danced around his subject. Finally, realising there was no way of couching his news in caveats, he spat it out.

"It's your father," he muttered. "I've heard he's going to be speaking up for Mary Chipperfield."

I had long felt let down by my father. He had cut me off. I had been disappointed that he had refused my invitations to come and visit Monkey World and was now sickened that he had decided to side with Mary Chipperfield over Trudy. My amateur psychologist's reading of the situation is that he had run a zoo that failed and was then jealous that I had become involved in a venture that was going from strength to strength. He was stuck in Shalford with a couple of stick insects and a garden snake in his front room, and he saw what was happening here from afar and this was a twisted form of revenge.

The case came to court the following January, 1999. I didn't go. I was too busy at the park. I read all about it, though, because it had become front-page news. The Chipperfields were an institution and, although circuses were falling out of favour and becoming an anachronism, Mary Chipperfield was a celebrity.

"On the film it is not hard to make out the screams of the chimpanzee," the prosecuting lawyer had told the court. The video was shown. There were gasps from the public gallery. Chipperfield was fined £7,500. She needed a police escort as she was led through a phalanx of angry animal rights protesters. They hurled abuse and chanted "Scum" as she sought refuge in the back of a police van. Chipperfield later said she felt like Myra Hindley. She received hate mail and recounted that one letter had been addressed to Cruella Chipperfield.

The fight for Trudy went on because Chipperfield initially refused to accept that Monkey World was the best place for the abused chimp. She said Trudy was her "baby" and should be returned because she was owned neither by her nor her husband, but by their company, Mary Chipperfield Promotions Limited.

That was a red rag to Jim. He made sure the media knew about the wrangle and that he was not prepared to let Trudy go back to a woman who had beaten her, forced her to live on biscuits and made her sleep in an unheated barn. It was not hard to muster support and it would have taken a very brave man to come down and take Trudy away from us. Her condition was improving, with Peggy now assuming the role of her surrogate mum, but the tips missing from her fingers and her introverted behaviour remained as evidence of the cruelty she had been subjected to.

We won the battle and the case did us a lot of good, not only in raising our profile, but also in making people realise that one of the real problems we faced was within Britain. A famous British firm had been caught with its pants down, not just some anonymous Spanish beach photographer. Suddenly, there was a realisation that British people were capable of carrying out this cruelty too. Given the awful cases we come across in the UK pet trade, this was a timely message.

I should add that I do not think that being involved in circus husbandry makes you a bad person. People have different ways of looking at things, different morals. Ten years ago, if you lived in Spain, it was safe for your kids to walk out on the streets after midnight, but it was also fine to keep chimpanzees in cupboards. Live in Britain and your kids couldn't go out for fear of being knifed, but you would get locked up for kicking your dog. It is a strange world. Historically, safari parks were often the object of some snobbery or bad feeling within the zoological world because they were often run by circus folk who had moved into a new line and hooked up with some wealthy landowner who needed to boost income on his estate. I just tried to stay clear of all such debates. I have my views on right and wrong, but preaching morality is fraught with problems. What is clear is that if you step over a legal line, the situation changes. That gives us something definite to work with. And that's what had happened with Trudy.

By now Jim was making contacts all over the world and the network throbbed with gossip and rumour about neglected animals. Word obviously got through to the powerbrokers in the TV world, because in 1998 the first series of *Monkey Business* was screened. This documentary programme followed the events at the park and was a huge hit with viewers. It ran for nine years and was shown on ITV as *Animal Planet* before it became *Monkey Life* and moved to Channel 5.

The programme has been great for the park and they

have recorded some great moments, but sometimes it could cause a few problems. I have come to understand that, when it comes to the media, nothing is more important than the programme or the newspaper, so inevitably there is the odd conflict. When an orang is being born, for instance, it is such a delicate, fragile thing that the last thing it needs is a TV crew with a great big arc light and cameras everywhere. A birth is stressful enough for an animal, so you try to make it as normal as you can. When Tom, Dick and Harry turn up in place of the usual familiar faces, it doesn't help. The animal knows something is up. I knew the programme was good for us, but there were times, for example when an animal was being anaesthetised, when it was the last thing we needed.

It also took a while to let them know that we could not delay things or do repeat shots. Animals do things when and if they want and so, if you want it on camera, you'd better be ready. I always called the directors Spielberg and found that the soundmen and cameramen were sometimes embarrassed by their airs and graces. That said, many of the crew became good friends and really came to care for and love the animals. And we are all grateful for the profile it has given our work.

Monkey Business helped spread the word about what

we were doing. From Spain to Dubai, we were becoming known. It had been the work of the Templers that had helped get us off the ground in the first place, and now we were about to forge another link that would grow stronger and stronger, and would see us take on Vietnamese smugglers and a modern-day King Kong.

15

Pingtung

KURTIS PEI IS a large Taiwanese man with a drive and desire that match his physique. He is in charge of the Pingtung Rescue Centre, which was designated a rescue centre after the Taiwan authorities brought in an act to clamp down on people keeping dangerous wild animals. Given the location, close to Indonesia, he was inundated with orang-utans. For me, Pingtung was manna from heaven.

There were several aims to Monkey World's partnership with Pingtung, including rehoming primates, investigating the chronic smuggling problem in Taiwan and providing veterinary support for them. I have been over there numerous times now and never cease to be impressed by Kurtis's appetite for life, both human and animal.

Blessed with an ability to party all night long, Kurtis is as mad as a snake and incredibly good fun, marrying a lust for life with his status as a very dedicated scientist who is held in high regard in every corner of Taiwan. The first time I went over there, I was greeted by a smiling face atop a giant's body. He took me back to Pingtung, where my eyes went through my eyebrows as he led me around the enclosures housing orangs, tigers, bears, birds of prey, reptiles and hundreds of Formosan macaques, an indigenous monkey.

There was rarely a dull moment with Kurtis. One day, he told me he was taking a trip as the Taiwanese people were going to hold hands and form a human chain all down the coast. The act was basically a V-sign to China. I am not a political man but I do have a natural sympathy for the underdog and so I said I would go too. Kurtis was as passionate about this as about his work. A deep-thinking, occasionally deep-drinking figure, he remains committed to the cause of neglected animals and people, and is a fount of all knowledge on the history and fate of the Taiwanese aborigines.

On one occasion, I was at Pingtung when Kurtis

got word that a shipment of illegal cargo had been confiscated from a Vietnamese boat. It was an achingly hot day with a cloudless sky. I was parched but ravenous with excitement when, later that afternoon, a rusting lorry creaked its way into the grounds of Pingtung.

I walked over with Kurtis and we were faced with a stack of blue containers of all shapes and sizes. I touched one and it scalded me. They were boiling in the heat and I feared for the contents. Someone trundled off and returned with a hose. We then sprayed the containers to keep them cool.

That was when the fun started. Once we had unloaded the containers, we started removing the lids. It was like Christmas for me. In one container would be a rare gibbon and in another a scorpion. There were scores of birds and all sorts of venomous snakes. We were in the tropics and so these containers could have housed anything. I would remove a lid, peer inside and, more often than not, slam the lid back down as I realised I was looking at a highly poisonous snake. All of them were very cheesed off too after travelling for so long in such horrible conditions.

Instead of heading for the pet and food trade, the cargo was rehomed, but it typified the problems facing Kurtis. He had an area roughly a third of the size of

Monkey World and was committed to providing for Taiwan's unwanted animals. That was what his funding was contingent upon, but he had more animals than he could cater for and so we would be a godsend to him.

The first orang-utan we took from him was RoRo. She was probably around 12 when she arrived and she had spent her life living in a cage in someone's kitchen. That was not unusual. The power of television was highlighted by the number of families who decided to buy orangs because of a popular sitcom called *The Naughty Family* in which an orang was kept as a house pet. Cute, cuddly and utterly divorced from reality, you might say this TV orang was the face that launched a thousand illegal cargo ships.

Everybody seemed to want an orang for a while, and there was a thriving pet trade as poachers shot and killed mothers and bundled the newly orphaned youngsters into rancid containers and rusting cages. RoRo was one of them, but she had been confiscated by the authorities.

I suspected Amy would not be the most welcoming of house-mates for her. Whether introducing Banghi to the laws of gravity or breaking the bullet-proof glass of her enclosure, she was a curmudgeon with a heart that she kept well hidden. Perhaps you could blame the surrogate mother for that.

Sure enough, Amy roused herself from her usual phlegmatic position to gnash her teeth and scream at RoRo. The poor girl had just travelled halfway round the world to be confronted with the vilest temper this side of Taiwan. RoRo fled to the farthest corner of the orang house while Amy asserted her authority as the Incredible Sulk. I separated the pair for a while as I plotted the next plan of action.

It was Gordon who took centre stage in this plan. Inquisitive and more passive than Amy, he adopted the role of peacemaker and approached RoRo with a refreshing absence of melodramatics. The pair quickly became good friends, although RoRo's superior size meant that Gordon would often find himself missing great clumps of orange fur after their wrestling bouts. When Amy witnessed this new-found bond, her mood worsened further. With the wronged expression of the finest Shakespearean actor, she flounced back to her quarters, turned her back and wallowed in her new role as victim.

As time went on, our link with Kurtis and other like-minded saviours around the globe strengthened. The following year Hsiao-quai and Lucky, an inappropriately named orang who had spent much of her life locked in an amusement arcade, arrived from Taiwan. Once again, the same chain of theatrics ensued before guards were dropped and the group agreed to co-exist. For me it was a joy to see us establishing a group of orangs, but there was one thing missing. Gordon was still an infant and we lacked a dominant male. I hoped that, in time, we could fill that void too and thus fulfil a lifelong dream of mine at the same time.

The trips abroad increased as we became part of a global network, and the days of making fibreglass rubbish bins in the shape of gorillas or sitting on West Bay beach in the wake of Taffy's demise seemed a long time ago. Life has an unfailing capacity to give with one hand and give you a clout with the other. Much like Amy, herself, in that respect.

One such overseas trip came about when Jim and Alison heard that the Jane Goodall Institute was having problems keeping some young chimps on a peninsula on Lake Tanganyika in Tanzania. Like an idiot, I had boasted that, such was our prowess with electric fences, I could even make one work in water. Boast delivered, I soon found myself on a four-seater plane flying at low altitude from Nairobi to Kigoma, with Terry Adams, Monkey World's resident fence builder, alongside me.

Looking out of the window, I was struck by the lack of habitat in Tanzania; I could count the number of trees I saw on the fingers of one hand. In addition, the only wildlife I saw as I scoured the scorched earth was a handful of birds gathered on a lake.

Everyone who works with wild animals has romantic views of Africa, but they were quickly brushed away by harsh reality as Terry and I sat by a makeshift train station in Kigoma, awaiting the materials to build our fence. I had already realised that Kigoma was afflicted by wall-to-wall poverty, with most people wearing nothing more than a hessian sack. The panoramic sky was pockmarked with huge clumps of shimmering black. I soon realised these blots on the skyscape were actually flies. The disease and poverty were humbling. As we clicked our heels, counting down the hours for the next train, hoping this one would be the one with our cargo, I noticed a gleaming white Land Cruiser drive through the squalor. On the side were the initials UN and inside was an intimidating figure. He would breeze through the slum and then depart. I may not do politics but the sight of all that spotless United Nations finery amid such misery was an eye-opener.

The train finally creaked into view amid a cloud of dust and mechanical wheezing. Terry and I got out of our Land Rover, which had already broken down several times, and awaited our booty. Before we were to get a glimpse of that, however, we were greeted by another stunning sight. The sides of the front few carriages were wrenched open and out piled a chain gang of prisoners, manacled together and bound for the neighbouring high-security jail. It was a scene straight out of the past as these convicts hobbled along, clanking and sweating under the fierce sun. I then almost gave Terry a heart attack by picking up my camera and taking a few shots.

"Christ, Jeremy!" he hissed. "You'll get us all locked up."

The train was also carrying our cargo, but it was not quite what I had been expecting. The fence posts were gnarled bits of chopped-down trees rather than the prefabricated stuff I had been used to. This was Africa. It was life stripped down to the bone, rubber nails and iron wood.

My task was tricky. I had to erect a fence some 20 metres out into the water and some six metres below the surface. The wires had to be taut and I had to maintain the voltage in any of the 15 wires above the surface. Bearing in mind that the tidal patterns meant the water level changed, this was a challenge. Someone managed to find me an old aqualung, and so I set about diving deep into the murky depths. I put a resistor on each wire so that when it earthed out, it was only that particular wire that was affected. It was taxing work but we did it. I am certainly not a miracle worker, but I like to say that while I can't walk on water, I can make an electric fence work in it.

We had a good team of helpers with us. We had little language in common other than some universal words like David Beckham and Manchester United. Aman, one of the local chaps, wore a bright red football shirt and confounded Terry and I with his knowledge of the beautiful game. I am no great football fan but was impressed that you could go into a place like Kitwe, isolated and seemingly rooted in the past, and find a man wearing a Manchester United shirt and pontificating on the club's history. I tried chatting with him about his life and we had a semblance of a conversation.

"So what do you do normally?" I asked him.

His eyes widened and a look of utter bemusement engulfed his face. He stared at me as if I had just crawled out from under a stone.

"I reeeelax," he said.

I often thought, afterwards, who has got it right?

I had the travelling bug then and still have it now. Africa would for evermore hold a special place in my heart, but it was Taiwan where I spent more of my time and it was there that I first heard about an almost mythical beast that was causing mayhem in Taichung City.

"Have you seen this?" Kurtis said one night as we looked at grainy pictures on a television screen. I squinted and saw video footage of two men lying ashen-faced in hospital beds. Both were cut and scarred and shrouded in bandages.

"What's happened?" I asked.

Kurtis kept his eyes on the screen.

"It's an orang," he responded. Then a pause. "A big one."

It quickly became clear that a large male orang was running amok in the city. People had been terrified as they saw this magnificent beast rampaging down the busy streets, dodging traffic and seeking refuge. What they did not realise was that he would have been more scared than all of the humans he encountered put together.

It was not hard to guess the big male's story. Born

in Borneo, raised in the treetops and orphaned when hunters shot his mother, he would have been sold into the pet trade and transported on one of the cramped death boats that did for so many orangs. Finally, he would have been bought by someone who was probably a fan of *The Naughty Family*. The cute factor no doubt paled as he grew in size and strength. Perhaps a daughter suddenly fell out of love with him when she realised he was not an obedient reality TV star but a dangerous wild animal.

So Tuan had fled. Somehow he had broken out of his cage – or maybe he was freed – and found himself wandering streets checkered with neon and danger. The locals had tried to capture him, but Tuan was strong and lashed out. Hence, the two men on drips and gurneys.

A team from Pingtung rushed to the location of the latest sighting, armed with enough ketamine to knock out four rhinos. They cornered him in a scrapyard. An oil drum was overturned. The team had nets and ropes and finally managed to tie him up. He was King Kong, a nasty, bad-tempered chap who felt, with due cause, that the world was against him.

It was in an atmosphere of considerable excitement that the truck containing Tuan rumbled into Pingtung some time later. I went to greet it with Kurtis. When the back of the truck was opened, Tuan shook the cage so violently that the entire thing fell out onto the floor with an iron thud.

"He's not happy," I mused, which was the ultimate in understatement.

They found a better crate for Tuan and made him comfortable for the night. That was no easy task. It involved marrying two crates, lashing them together with secure bindings and then opening the door. When Tuan lumbered through, the sliding door was closed instantly. Jim and Alison were also there, as enthralled by the spectacle as I was. Kurtis's team worked to get Tuan's enclosure ready for him. Although he was, indeed, a large male, he was not exceptional and Pingtung had others of a similar bulk. It just went to show how the media and the grapevine can paint distorted images.

I felt this was my time, my fun time, and I had no intention of just sitting back and watching as an interested onlooker. So the next morning, when the others were still sleeping, I went back to see Tuan. I am the only keeper at Monkey World who will go in with the orangs, and sometimes Jim and Alison would suggest I had some sort of magic power. When they arrived later that day and saw me holding hands with Tuan through the two-inch-thick railings, their view was reinforced. The truth was far simpler than that. All I did was hang out with Tuan and make friends with him. He fixed me with his suspicious eyes, the memory of the previous night no doubt festering, but I started speaking in a low voice.

"Come on, mate, what's your problem?" I started. "What's all the fuss about. You're okay." I let him mumble his defiance and then added: "Have you finished?"

I quickly found that if you were like that with Tuan, you could win him over. I spent a lot of time with him and before long we were getting on fine. He had never encountered anything but people poking him with sticks, shooting his mother and generally being horrible to him. He had every right to be on his guard and defensive, but I was nice to him, so his distrust slowly ebbed away. It is for this reason that I always carry a packet of Polos with me. They are an ice-breaker and deal-maker. Give someone a sweet and they will be your friend. It's not magic or rocket science.

Kurtis had more male orangs than you could shake a stick at, so I saw an opportunity with Tuan.

"How the hell did you do that?" Jim said after seeing

me holding hands with this big ape. He was impressed and happy. It was a good time.

"I want him on the next shipment, Jim."

"Okay."

"I mean it. I want him."

We were already committed to taking animals from Kurtis. They had more animals coming in than they had space for, so it was not that difficult to persuade Kurtis. Another large male orang was not quite the novelty for him that it was for us. The deal was done. With a word rather than money. To do anything else would have been against our principles.

We returned home to Dorset and I was delighted by the thought of having Tuan join us. There was much to do beforehand. The first thing we always do is make sure that any animal who is coming to Monkey World is medically clean. That involves John Lewis giving all newcomers a check-up. Any rescue also involves myriad steps and, although we had already done the initial assessment, there was the usual library of paperwork and politics to overcome. We have to ask if the animal is protected by CITES, the Convention on the International Trade in Endangered Species, and if the country the animal is being rescued from abides by its own rules. The site management team must also get the infrastructure ready back at Monkey World. Meanwhile, my primate care team and I ensure conditions within any particular group are right for the newcomer. Even with a straightforward case like Tuan, where we knew his background and the good people at Pingtung, it would take a year before we were ready for him.

When John did give the all-clear, I felt a surge of excitement, but the mission to bring him back was fraught with problems. We took a circuitous route as there were other calls of mercy to be answered. Then things took another twist in Taipei. I was lying in my hotel there and was just drifting off to sleep when I heard a siren outside. For some reason, I just knew that it was significant. Call it a sixth sense or whatever. I listened to the rise and fall of the siren and, within a few minutes, the phone went.

"Jeremy, it's Alison. Jim's collapsed!"

I leapt out of bed, threw on some clothes and rushed out. Jim had been suffering from incredible head pains and was now in the back of an ambulance on his way to hospital attached to an IV drip. They had him on Valium overnight and he stayed in the next day too. Luckily, he was so out of it that he did not notice the awful scene around him. It really was a third-world hospital with the dead and dying lying in every available space. Jim was totally neurotic about such matters and I am sure he would have felt considerably worse had he known where we were. It is fair to say that Jim could be a real liability with his health.

Finally, Kurtis came and collected us and we went to Pingtung. It was good to see Tuan again. Some male orangs are just plain nasty, but he isn't one of those. I had bonded with him more than a year earlier and the ties had only strengthened during my absence.

Once again, we seemed to live a charmed life when it came to transporting our animals. Ever since I had taken Gordon Mills's apes to America all those years ago, the airlines had usually let us stay in the hold. That is useful as regards their physical health and security, but the main advantage is for their emotional well-being. The fact is flying can be a traumatic experience for animals. The way I explain it is by saying that you would not put a three-year-old child on a 20-hour flight and just pick him up at the other end, so why would you do it with an orang-utan? That is why I had flown to Taiwan and hung out with Tuan for a week beforehand, rebuilding bridges and calming his nerves.

Sometimes we give the apes a sedative, but it is better to avoid that if you can because there is always a chance of them inhaling vomit or having a seizure. You try to get by with kind words and friendly faces, but transporting animals is always problematic. I knew that from the time I had worked at Colchester Zoo with Frank Farrah and we had been moving a tiger. I can still recall our anxious glances and sweaty brows as Frank stuffed zoo leaflets into the holes that the tiger was eating in the crate behind him. That was quite fun. It certainly persuaded Frank to put his foot down.

Tuan's trip was comfortable, though, and it was not long before it was time to introduce him to his new cohabitants. There is always some handbagging to start with, but that's all it is. Any more serious issues, such as bullying, will evolve over time. We introduce a new animal to his new house-mates one by one. The trick is to get the dominant animal onside. If you do that, the battle is won, as a junior-ranking animal might think, "I'd really like to beat the hell out of him, but I don't want to get on the wrong side of the boss." Meanwhile, the dominant animal will use the newcomer as a badge of honour and will put on a bit of a display as if to warn the others that they had best leave him alone. As in every walk of life, it's good to have a decent leader.

The fact is you simply cannot put two grown-up

male orangs together, as they would fight each other to the point of death. However, it is different if there is a significant age gap: Tuan had no problem with Gordon because he was still an infant. The only exception to this rule in my experience has been when two animals have grown up together, like Coco and Louis during my days at Little Rhondda. But even then there came a time when Coco started bullying his former friend. The normal thing in those circumstances is to punish the bad guy, but the problem with orangs is that they are solitary animals anyway, and so isolating them is scarcely a stiff punishment. For a chimp it would be the most terrible measure, but an orang merely sits on his own and shrugs, "Whatever." I think this will probably be the nail in the coffin of keeping the orang in captivity. With chimps there is a defined hierarchy and they live together in self-sustaining harmony; with orangs you need a new enclosure for every grown male and that is a big price to pay for an animal that will not move unless there is food or a woman involved.

The difficulty with Tuan's introduction was not another male but his jealous women. Amy and Lucky both wanted this hunk of manliness and he was happy to oblige. Tuan had different relationships with the duo. Lucky was his blue-eyed girl, but not particularly for sexual reasons, and he treated her like a youngest daughter, albeit a highly possessive one. Appreciating this, Amy would wind up Lucky by reaching out and touching Tuan every so often. It would be enough to turn Lucky green-eyed with envy.

Nevertheless, it was not long before things settled down and Tuan and Amy mated. In fact, that was Gordon's downfall. Intrigued by the grunting of the rutting beasts, he wandered over and, being Gordon, had an opinion. Tuan is a nice guy, but everyone needs a degree of privacy, so he clouted him. Gordon was unabashed and came back for more, wondering what was happening to his mother. That was when Tuan snapped and inadvertently bit him. The result was a damaged eye. Along with his Fu Manchu beard, this remains Gordon's distinctive mark.

With Tuan settled in, though, we had a proper group of orang-utans on our derelict pig farm. For me it was the end of a journey that had started when I had force-fed Amy through those stormy nights of yore. Finally, the old girl was part of a family. It felt good.

16

Indelible Marks

THE FIRST TATTOO I ever got was a Chinese dragon. The last one was the vine that goes all the way up my right leg. One day, I was having lunch in the café with John Lewis and I asked him what animals I could include in the design.

"A slug," he suggested.

"A slug," I replied. "Good idea."

Hence, I now have a slug and a tree frog on my leg, but the most notable tattoo I have is the large hooded orang-utan on my right forearm. That is RoRo dressed as the Grim Reaper. I realise that sounds very morbid, but I have always felt she has a gloomy face and she certainly lived up to the billing on one occasion many years earlier when she had left another indelible mark, this time on Jim.

It was 2000, a new millennium, and although we were never more than one calamity away from disaster and even closure, the park was thriving. Our reputation had spread and that meant Jim was often locked away in the office, dealing with the politics that always needed wading through before any rescue could happen.

I felt for him. To me, Jim got the raw end of the deal. This was all about animals and our shared passion for primates, but it must have been easy to forget that when burning the midnight oil, all tangled up in red tape. To cheer him up, every so often I would take Jim in with the apes. It was a pick-me-up and a reminder of what it was all about. Unfortunately, reality can sometimes bite too hard.

"Do you fancy going in with the orangs?" I asked.

Jim's enthusiasm was instant. "Yeah, that'd be great."

"Okay, let's try RoRo and Gordon."

I took Jim and Alison into the cage. Cue Bedlam. For some reason, RoRo jumped on Jim and pinned him to the floor. I am sorry to say that through personal experience I have garnered a great knowledge of the different ways apes attack. A gorilla will run at you, bash you very hard, bite and run off. A chimp will stand over you in a state of hysteria until it has got over it and will then go and do something else. An orang, however, has more dexterity than both. It has four very capable hands and it will fasten one on each of your limbs. Immediately, I jumped on RoRo and managed to prise her off. Jim was pretty shaken up. Why did it happen? I think you can overanalyse these things. The fact is it did. RoRo is an ape. Like the time when Coco did the same to me back at Little Rhondda, you have to expect the unexpected. On another occasion, when visiting Pingtung, an orang got hold of John Lewis, the vet, as he walked past the cage. It was throttling John when I managed to separate them. They are strange beasts.

A lot of people have been hurt by orangs, gorillas and chimps, whether it be me, John or the two Taiwanese men put in hospital by Tuan, but there is no record of them killing people. You have to treat them with respect and not let any intimacy or friendship blind you to their wildness. They are like us, really. If the bachelor boys in Butch's chimp group fought, it was no different from behaviour I had seen in my my own parents' marriage. And if mothers like Amy abandoned babies, it was born of their being wrenched from the wild while their own mothers were murdered for meat or money. Their behaviour was a product of their history, which goes for most of us. We do things partly by instinct and partly by example.

Man still takes the biscuit when it comes to inflicting the most grievous cruelty. I found that out when I travelled to Pingtung again in July 2001. We took a circuitous route and first went to Phuket to deliver some special pellets to a gibbon rescue centre named Highland Farm. Then we travelled to another sanctuary on the Burmese border run by an eccentric American guy, Bill, and his wife. They had gibbons, bears, big cats and, like all of us, struggled with funds, but they lived in a state of additional peril. One day over an al-fresco breakfast, Bill told us that customs had seized a massive haul of drugs that was coming over the border. A gunfight had ensued and 15 people had been killed.

"Where was this?" I asked him.

Bill slurped his coffee and waved a hand casually to my left.

"About 200 yards down there," he said.

"Oh, right," I said, nervously picturing the slaughter.

Travelling the world never fails to open my eyes to how people live, and the dangers that were so casually dismissed by our American host would be brought home in a horrific fashion the following year when we heard that both he and the lovely four-year-old daughter of one of his staff had been shot dead.

Cruelty crosses all borders. Back in 2000, Lulu arrived at Monkey World. She is a firm favourite with our visitors, but few probably appreciate quite what she has been through; they just know her as the chimp with one arm.

Lulu was born in a Russian circus travelling through Cyprus. Shortly after she was born, her mother bit her very badly. It left a nasty wound and she was in a chronic condition, but the circus was loath to spend money on treating her. Luckily, a family visited the circus one night and asked if they could help. A deal was done and Lulu went home with them. The family contacted their local vet and he amputated Lulu's right arm. She was so young that it is unlikely it had any notable effect on her.

However, her background did. Separated from her mother and living an itinerant life, Lulu was a mess of problems. She attacked the woman who had saved her and broke the family television set. For all their good intentions, the family realised they were not going to be able to deal with such an angry chimp and so, with Lulu now housed in their stables, the call came through to us.

She was given tea and toast and marmalade when she arrived at Heathrow Airport, but she struggled to settle in with the other chimps in Dorset. I wondered how disabled she would be because of her missing limb, but any doubts about that were laid to rest when I saw her perform the most fantastic flying drop-kick on another chimp. Even without an arm, she could punch you in the mouth, and her climbing skills were utterly unaffected.

The difficulty was that she did not associate with the other chimps and that presented a very basic but irritating problem. I put her in with Sally's group, but when the others charged out for breakfast each morning shouting, "Eureka!", Lulu stayed put.

"Come on, girl," I would say. "There's a nice bit of grub out there."

She would cross her arms and almost raise her eyebrows, as if to say, "I'm not coming."

It took me months and months to convince her to go outside and that the world would not end if she did. She steadfastly refused to be blackmailed with food and, to this day, remains the most efficient animal in the world, with an ability to survive on three grapes a week. I racked my brains and was at my wits' end when one day – no different to all the others – she got up and walked outside.

From that moment on she decided that the past was history and she was actually an outside girl. Now I could never get her to go back inside. Her house had three bedrooms with two doors that opened onto the outside of the enclosure. In the summer I opened them all up, but in the winter I would have only one door ajar. All the others would merrily come through that door and go to bed. All apart from Lulu. With her, I would have to let the others in, shut that door, walk all the way around the enclosure and then open the other door. Then, if Lulu felt like it – and it was a big if – she would deign to enter the house.

I still spend a lot of my time outside the chimps' enclosure saying, "Come on, Lulu, are you coming to bed or what?" She just likes the drama. Having been almost agoraphobic when she arrived, she now craves the outdoor life. When it rains I toss her a blanket, which she will use to shield herself from the wet and then, almost without fail, use to jam the sliding door. Again, people try to analyse such behaviour and ask why she does it. The answer is because she can. It's a control thing. It's what makes the world go round and I love her for it.

By the time Lulu arrived, our reputation had grown even further – we were well known the world over. It was hard to imagine, given our humble beginnings, but we were gaining respect from people who mattered. One area of particular expertise was with woolly monkeys. They are the most delicate of creatures and are very hard work. They suffer a lot from high blood pressure and tension and have the most particular dietary requirements. I often remind our staff that our animals are not "bleeding gourmets" and that if a gibbon does not have his daily dose of grapes, it won't kill him.

"Just give them those plums we got given free," I say. "It's a gibbon, not Raymond Blanc."

Woolly monkeys are different, though. They eat a low-grade leaf diet in the wild, but they need more quality in England to keep them warm and healthy. It becomes a case of juggling trial and error, but it is so perilous that many zoos have given up on them. That was why Marina, my co-keeper, and I went back to Howletts Zoo that August to pick up their entire collection.

For me it was a trip down memory lane and I pointed out the now revamped shack where I had first been seduced by Jim's pipe-dream. I passed the fruit shed where I had kept Amy while attending to my duties, and my mind wandered back to the trip I had taken with her which ended up in a wreck by the side of the M2. I was brought back to the present by the sight of the monkeys. I now feel a tinge of pride at how we have coped with this difficult species; we even have Xuzy, who is officially the oldest woolly monkey in the world.

A couple of weeks later, Peggy gave birth to Ben. This was another accident, as many of our chimp births have been. Peggy, named after Peggy Templer, was one of the dominant females. The baby arrived at 3.15pm and Peggy nibbled at the placenta before putting him down and leaving him alone. She was just another example of a neglected child having no idea how to be a mother. Lee, one of our keepers, distracted her while I darted in and picked up Ben. The TV guys filmed this and it would almost give Jim a heart attack when he saw it. I wrapped Ben in a blanket and took him back to the bungalow, where he was put in an incubator. All those years on from Amy and I now had another house guest.

Not long afterwards, on Jim's birthday, Cherri had a baby, Pip, after managing to remove her birth control implant. Cherri had already been on the coil and the pill, but had also produced Seamus. Now she showed signs of wanting to care for Pip, but kept putting her down to wander off to play. I rang Jim, who was with Alison in California for Christmas, to discuss plans to hand-rear her. We always make decisions on such matters collectively. I went into the enclosure and Cherri climbed onto me. I walked away with her clinging to my back, while Lee and Dave opened the far door and removed Pip. And so the process began again. We have been very fortunate that all of our chimp mistakes seem to have come in twos and that makes it much easier to raise them, because if they see what another chimp is like in the early days, it does not come as such a shock when they are reintroduced to the others.

I often get asked about the character of different species. It is possible to make generalisations, but that is all they are. Each individual animal has different characteristics. We have lovely, fun chaps and miserable old sods. This is part of life's rich pageant. Many people might wonder just what I see in Amy, who is a gruff, solitary soul with a chip on both shoulders, but we have been through so much and known each other for so long that there will always be something special between us.

I took Ben and Pip from my house into Monkey World proper for the first time that same week. The old ape nursery was in the visitor centre, so they stayed there for the day and then came back with me at night. It was an ongoing process, a slow act of acclimatising them to new surroundings and getting them used to their future family. It would be the following year before we introduced Ben and Pip to two other chimps, Seamus and Johni. They played well and I was relieved. Maybe I'd brought these two up well.

These introductions are hugely satisfying but fraught with potential mishaps, as was the case when we introduced Johni into Paddy's group. As usual on such days, I turned up at the cage armed with a blow pipe and an anaesthetic dart. Johni wandered into the enclosure and Jimmy went for her. Something had irked him, so he flew at the newcomer with arms flailing and teeth bared. Poor old Johni must have wondered what had hit her. As must Jimmy when the dart thudded into him. I breathed deeply. Darting is always a risk, but I managed to pull off a dead-eye Dick shot. Luckily for us, John Lewis was at the park that day and was able to sew up Johni's wounded foot.

On July 8, I made a brief note in my diary: "Mother died."

It sounds harsh, I know, but my philosophy is that if I cannot be bothered to see you when you are alive, then the same goes for when you are dead. And there were good reasons for this. My mother was an extraordinary woman, but some of her treatment of me was simply appalling. At this point, I was still burdened with the baggage from my childhood and I would not be able truly to reconcile myself to my past until much later. After my car crash, I had needed to get the events from my past into a straight line in order to understand them. But as I kept confronting certain memories – what had happened and why – I became increasingly unhappy that some of them had been put to bed. I was not comfortable with the past, and the one thing I was waiting for before I confronted it properly was my mother's death. I know it sounds callous but I thought that would change things. It didn't. The last time we had spoken was many months before and she had once again flown into a rage for some reason. She was cremated on July 11. I didn't go.

I had other things to think about. Monkey World was now a huge, sprawling site and we had successful groups of orangs and chimps, as well as the chimp

252

nursery and all the other monkeys to cater for. It was an all-consuming task, leaving little time for a social life or holidays, but I loved it. If I owe my parents anything, it is that I was fortunate to have grown up in an environment that exposed me to the wonders of the natural world. My real family now was Jim and Alison, Tuan and Amy, Ben and Pip. We all counted on each other in a way I had never done with my blood relatives.

Soon after my mother's death, I went back to Pingtung. I had spoken with Chantz, the head keeper, about returning to make the cages safer. So, armed with a bag of tools, 20 galvanised water bowls, a toothbrush and some other materials, I departed for southern Taiwan.

The first job I undertook was to free and renovate a sliding door on one of the tiger enclosures. This door had been left unused in the open position for some years and needed excavating, freeing and lubricating. I welded the handle and made a new locking mechanism. That was my first day gone.

The top priority, though, was to create a better quarantine home for a female orang-utan who had recently arrived at the centre. When new individuals arrive at the centre, it is critical that they are kept separate for quarantine until the vets have been able to run all the tests that ensure that the new monkey or ape is healthy. The quickest and most practical option was to weld two large steel cages together in a manner that would fit in the quarantine building. Mae the orang-utan appeared happy with the results. Over the next few days, I got out my welding gun to make other areas safer. Previously, they had cages where adult male orang-utans and tigers could reach through the cages and potentially grab unsuspecting keepers, vets, or visitors – as John had found to his cost.

I returned home enthused by the work being done in Pingtung and Chantz's gratitude. I suited a life among waifs and strays, the runts and the rejected. I was constantly dealing with the diseased and disabled. There was Beth and her missing foot. The story went that the bullet that killed her mother also got her. Then there was Mona, the stunted chimp with the curved spine and malformed hips, a relic of her days living in a box, drugged up on Valium. In addition to those problems, Mona had cataracts in both eyes. We looked into the prospect of having them removed but decided it just was not viable. The operation itself was not dangerous, but when you have lens replacement it itches like hell and you must not rub your eyes for a number of weeks. Quite how you tell a chimp to refrain from doing that was beyond us. So Mona soldiered on, a totem for the perils of the beach photography trade and the work we were doing. It was a battle that would be won the following year.

17

The Last Chimp

ALBERTO WAS A big male adult chimpanzee and the end of an era. He had been used as a beach photographer's prop but, thanks to the campaigning zeal of Jim and Alison, the practice had been outlawed. The photographer struck a deal with the Guardia Civil by which he would keep Alberto as a pet instead. Later, when his owner died, he ended up at a cat's home. Cue a mercy call from an organisation called Depana, permits from the Ministry of Agriculture and, on February 19, 2003, the arrival of the last beach chimp.

Alberto travelled light but came with a lot of emotional baggage. He was very aggressive and very difficult to introduce to the resident chaps. Deep down, he was a nice bloke, but he was so hard, one of the hardest animals I had ever met. He wanted to be top dog and was prepared to scrap and fight for the honour.

The bachelor boys were in good voice when he arrived, excited to find out who was in the box that was being transported through the park and into the bedrooms. Alberto, too, was no doubt curious about the noise outside and the shadowy figures moving around in the dimming light.

I quickly realised Alberto had a problem with a broken finger. It had clearly become detached a while before and was left dangling in an awkward way. John Lewis came down and looked at the rogue digit.

"It's going to have to come off," he said.

"If you don't do it, then the other chimps will," I added.

"Yes. No option."

The surgery was a success, but Alberto was still taking time to get used to his new surroundings. He had always been on his own and, although that is unnatural for a chimp, it was all he had known and he was habituated to that mode of living. That night he wrecked his bedroom, tossing toys, bedding and food around and managing to break the sliding door. I got my welder out again and wondered if we were fighting a losing battle with him.

He was on his own for a long time before we decided to risk an introduction. In the interim we had his teeth done. Peter Kertesz is the founder of Zoodent, an organisation specialising in dental care in animals, and he came down to the park for one of his occasional visits. Whenever Peter visited, we worked him into the ground, starting him at 6am and sometimes not finishing until the wee small hours of the following morning. He was the best and we were determined to get the best out of him. Alberto was one of those who needed some work done and Peter obliged.

I stuck with my time-honoured technique of trying to get the boss to accept any newcomer. Hence, Butch was first on my list of chimps to meet Alberto. They looked at each other through the mesh in the back bedrooms of the pavilions for a while. Alberto bristled with masculinity and reared up to his full intimidating height. Butch, a tough leader, seemed less convinced without the aid of his trusty henchmen. The door slid back. In a flash of fur and fury, they went for each other, with Alberto clearly the chief aggressor. I hit the fire extinguisher that I was holding for just this eventuality and doused them both with a stream of water. That distracted them and they ran off in opposing directions.

We stuck with this plan because Butch was the leader of the bachelor group. Most days I would put them together in the bedrooms, the large playroom or the outdoor enclosure. I expanded the climbing frame and made new tunnels so that both would have escape routes should things turn nasty. It worked. The duo chased each other around but increasingly interspersed their duels with long rests. Gradually, they developed a small semblance of tolerance, but neither was prepared to step down. Butch ultimately dug deep to see off Alberto, but the newcomer was a belligerent brute if he did not like you. If you'd been scoring the duel, it would have been a long-running draw.

It was time to try another introduction, so we brought in Jestah, one of the former Windsor Safari Park chimps who suffered from occasional bouts of eczema but was hard as old boots. I noted that, despite the shouting, she and Alberto didn't kill each other during their 45-minute summit meeting. Soon afterwards, I let them spend two hours together. It was a softly-softly approach and a slow season of little victories.

Worse was to follow. Mojo had been another Valium addict when he pitched up from Spain and he generally kept himself to himself. I decided to try Alberto with Mojo and Rocky, with a mesh separating them. Mojo was clearly terrified by this large, aggressive beast and shrunk away. Rocky, living up to his name, was more curious. However, when Alberto stuck his tongue out at him through the mesh of his enclosure, it was Mojo who was sufficiently roused to bite off the end. I called Mike Nathan, another great vet we used, and he came down. Alberto, cool as you like, approached us and showed us his new wound. Mike pulled out a pair of scissors and trimmed the tongue. Alberto did not even wince. Like I said, he was an amazingly tough individual and I warmed to him because of that. He was not namby-pamby like some. Alberto was made of stern stuff.

By now I had moved to Grants Farm, a half-mile up the track, hidden by the trees that shroud Monkey World. I rode to work on a quad bike and loved that early morning trip, the dawn chorus of bird and, occasionally, chimp song ringing in my ears. Slowly, things began to move towards happy conclusions. By July 2003, Ben and Pip were getting on fine with Seamus and Johni. Alberto, meanwhile, was introduced to

Sammy and we made a vital breakthrough. Sammy is a pretty tough lad, as evinced by the scars from having cigarettes stubbed out on his head, but likes a quiet life. You would not mess with him, but he opts out of office politics and does not want any grief. I noted that during their first meeting, Alberto was in attack mode, but they had three hours together. It was a big step forwards.

With so many chimps at Monkey World, it was always a case of swings and roundabouts. So as Alberto settled in, I noticed that Johni had a curious lump on her back. I am not an expert, but lumps are rarely good, so John came to take a look.

"That's a bit mysterious," he said. "I'd better take a biopsy."

Johni was soon given an anaesthetic and John took his sample. It turned out to be a carcinoma.

"It's going to have to come off," John said.

"What are her chances?"

"It's an unusual sort. Dangerous. The chances are it will come back."

It's always hard when you hear bleak news about animals you have cared for and bonded with, but you carry on with your routine and hope for the best. And there was always something to divert your attention. That September, Alberto was back in the thick of it as Butch bit his finger down to the bone. That is what chimps do. People subscribe to the image that they are the cutest things, but they can also be anything but. Alberto had his finger rerooted and carried on. He had lost one finger, part of his tongue and now had another crushed digit. It could be a hard life with the bachelor boys.

As another year drew to a close, it was the orangs who began to take up my attention. RoRo was pregnant and we were eagerly anticipating the second birth at the park. Whereas we tried to control the birth of chimps, orangs were endangered and we were part of an international breeding programme with our colleagues at Pingtung. Gordon was alive and thriving, and despite Amy's suspect maternal instincts, we were confident we could have more babies.

I fixed up CCTV in RoRo's house so that we would not miss anything and waited. I did not have to wait long. The birth went well and I found RoRo tucked up with her tiny baby one morning. I watched them for several hours, hoping to see the maternal instinct that had been missing in Amy. RoRo had already cut the umbilical cord and cleaned the baby, but she held her facing away from her, meaning it would be impossible for her to suckle. Then I watched as RoRo grabbed a blanket and wrapped the baby in it. She was doing her best, but her mother had been murdered and she had not been able to pass on any tips on raising babies. RoRo clearly thought the baby was a toy, so she would have to be removed. I had already done so by the time Mike Colbourne arrived. I looked at Mike with a resigned expression and he knew what was coming.

"She's not going to feed," I told him. "No option. I've already got the incubator going."

It was decided that Mike should be the foster mum this time and he took the baby to her new on-site home. She weighed in at 1.78kg and Mike gave her boiled water and a rehydration powder. Soon she would move on to milk with a quarter-strength formula so that it would not be too rich for her digestive system. Within two months, she was taking 350 millilitres of milk a day. Her teeth began to come through and that put her off suckling on the teat of a bottle, but Mike rubbed some Bonjela onto her gums to ease the pain.

By October 20 she had grown to a mighty 2.5kg. It was satisfying for all of us. RoRo had been the first orang to come to the park from Pingtung, followed by Lucky, Hsiao-quai and Tuan. That she should be the first mother as part of our breeding programme with Pingtung seemed fitting. Orangs are still struggling terribly in the wild and many experts estimate that they will be extinct within 10 years. I try to deal with the day-to-day reality and, while some people have said that if an animal is unable to survive on its own merits in the wild then it should be left to die, I cannot help thinking it is our duty to preserve these wonderful animals. Orangs could survive quite happily, but their habitat is being destroyed by the palm oil and logging industries. In addition, the great apes are hunted for meat. Poachers know they can get two-for-one deals with orangs as, when the mother is shot dead and the carcass sold as an illegal delicacy, the newly orphaned baby will cling to the mother's chest. The babies can then be dumped in baskets and smuggled into the pet trade. This will no doubt have been RoRo's traumatic start in life.

Soon after RoRo had become a mother, Vivien Lin, Kurtis's right-hand woman from the Pingtung Rescue Centre, came to Monkey World to see the baby and observe how she was cared for. There was a discussion about names.

"I think a good name would be Hsiao-ning," she said. "That means peaceful sunrise."

"Seems fitting as it's the start of our partnership," Mike said.

Jim and Alison were happy.

"Fine by me," I added, although I knew that there was rarely anything peaceful about life at Monkey World.

I began to feel luckier by the end of the year. Johni's cancer did not come back, and then I went to Pingtung and had the experience of a lifetime. I was upstairs in the staff area overlooking the enclosures and the corrugated-iron shelter that housed the scores of bikes that the university staff rode in on every day. At first I didn't notice anything, but gradually I had a nagging awareness that something wasn't right. It was hard to put my finger on it at first, but it was as if something was out of synch, something just out of kilter with normality. Chantz evidently felt the same.

"Do you hear that?" he muttered over lunch.

I listened hard but couldn't hear anything.

"What?" I asked.

"Exactly."

Things clicked into place. At Pingtung, just as at Monkey World, the air often reverberated with cries and calls. It was a riot of noise, from the orangs calling through their throat sacs to the baritone growl of the tigers. Yet now there was just a deathly silence. It was as if time was suspended. Then I looked out of the window and noticed the long iron shelter physically swaying. There was a dreadful rumble deep down in the building and the crockery began to shake.

"It's an earthquake!" Chantz cried.

We dived for cover and waited until it had passed. Later, watching the news and talking to Chantz, I would find out that we had felt the aftershock of an earthquake to the north-east of Taidung. It registered seven on the Richter Scale and was very exciting. Given that we were surrounded by tigers, orangs and the rest, I realised how serious the repercussions could have been. We checked the enclosures but the tremors had not been enough to wreck my previous handiwork. I was reassured and felt a tinge of pride, but then remembered how the animals had mysteriously fallen silent just before the quake. It made me realise that animals really do know more than us.

18
Alice

My world was still shaking in 2004 when early in the year, Mel, my fourth wife, left me. It was another disappointment as all failed marriages are. I would never be mean-spirited about my ex-wives, but am always reminded of the words of the great Walker Brothers song: "There's no regrets, no tears goodbye, I don't want you back, we'd only cry again."

I don't buy this idea that you can love someone enough to marry them and then feel no affection for them at all when it is over. I could never understand my father, who loathed my mother to his dying day even though he hadn't seen her for many years. Shame on you if you feel like that. You try and if you fail, you move on. No regrets.

That does not mean that it is easy to deal with and I was glad to have Ben and Pip to occupy my time and act as a diversion as we continued to introduce them to more folk. Then, one day as I passed by the orang house, I noticed that Hsiao-quai had the tell-tale grape swellings. There was no doubt. She was pregnant. I jotted down the date and tried to work out the ETA as close as I could.

Thereafter the year descended into a long series of kicks in the teeth. The first came when Rodney died. He had struggled to impose himself and came off worse when Hananya launched an overthrow. Hananya was a nice enough chap, but he was young to be a leader and, without wishing to be unkind, not the sharpest tool in the box, favouring brawn over brain. It was terribly sad to see Rodney go, and the pain of his passing was exacerbated two months later when Mona dropped dead. With all her manifold problems, it was easy to have a soft spot for Mona, but her past meant she was never likely to live a long life. Like they say, the good really do die young.

And then my world really was shaken to its

foundations. A woman whom I had dated briefly back in the days when I lived on Gordon Mills's estate got in touch and said she wanted to buy me a car. After two decades apart, it seemed a bizarre offer, but I was driving around in an old wreck held together by hope and rust, so finally I gave in and was stunned when the Toyota RAV4 was delivered to me that Christmas.

Slowly the truth filtered out. The woman had had a child after our affair and never told me. The child was called Alice. When she was only two, Alice had been diagnosed with leukaemia and had died. The woman showed me photographs and I was consumed by a mix of conflicting emotions – joy at seeing this beautiful little girl, misery at knowing I would never see her in the flesh, horror at what had happened to her. I am not knocking the mother for keeping it a secret as there is nothing as unique to a person as their own morals, but all I can say is I would have had a problem with remaining silent if the boot had been on the other foot.

The car was obviously the result of some festering guilt. I handed over some hair so she could do a DNA test. It was positive. She told me what had happened and then we drove down to the little village in Cornwall where Alice was buried. It was a strange and horrible thing to be grieving for someone I had never known and who had been dead for 20 years, but it felt as raw as if it had happened that day.

I was glad to get away the following January when John Lewis and I went to Taiwan to pick up an orange person named A-mei. We estimated that she was about 10 years old and we were encouraged to hear that she had cared for a baby that she had had during her time at Pingtung, although it had ultimately died. Chantz was pleased to see us, but gave us a damning impression of our newcomer.

"She is a very nasty monkey," he spat out in his clipped vowels. "Spiteful! Very spiteful!" He shrugged his shoulders. "I can't do anything for her."

Chantz was glad to see John as he said we would need to anaesthetise A-mei to move her into her travelling crate. I was glad John was there too. Anaesthesia is a dangerous business: that's why we always have a vet on hand whenever we need to use it back at the park. It is vital to get the dosage just right. John was the best and so we had made the long journey to Taiwan together.

I made a docking device and rigged the new crate up to the side of A-mei's enclosure so she could get used to it for a few days. Whereupon A-mei – this terribly nasty, spiteful monkey – got up, walked into the new crate and sat down, a picture of utter contentment. At least John had the decency to laugh. He would not be required after all. I quickly gelled with A-mei and we became firm friends. Although there was no need for a dart or a veterinary expert, John did manage to put himself to good use by doing some dental work on a Pingtung gibbon. Chantz scratched his head.

A-mei would go on to have a unique role at Monkey World. Much like Sally the chimp, she struggled to fit in when she arrived and the other females did not take to her. However, a job opportunity as resident foster mum that was perfect for A-mei's good nature would soon arise.

We were proud of the way we were rearing babies and it was not long before we became home to Europe's only orang-utan crèche, meaning we had a place for the babies born in the park and also those from other zoos. Aris arrived from Stuttgart with his German keepers, who came over to make sure he settled in. He was a will-o-the-wisp with a cut above an eye. That was a result of a bite from his grandmother, who had cared for him after he was rejected by his mother. The grandmother was also looking after Aris's uncle at the time, and when it became too much she lashed out. So Aris ended up in the German ape nursery with a bunch of baby gorillas. He was only tiny, but it was fair to say he had already done lots of living. I put him in with Hsiao-ning and was delighted to find they got on fine. They were of a similar age and I was quietly confident, but you can never get too cocky in this world or something will come along to bite you on the backside.

At 2pm on March 15, Hsiao-quai went into labour. The contractions continued and then at 2.41 her waters broke. The head appeared at 3.04, and the baby was delivered at 3.06. From the time of the first contraction, the birth went very quickly, which is unusual for a first-time mother.

Throughout the labour, Hsiao-quai remained very tolerant of my presence and seemed to appreciate the encouragement I was giving her. I was allowed to film the entire birth and, when the baby's head first appeared, Hsiao-quai let me remove the mucus that was in the infant's mouth. From the moment the baby was born, Hsiao-quai was attentive, cleaning the baby head to toe, carefully removing the cord and gently handling the infant while supporting its head. Somehow Tuan, the father of the new arrival, knew exactly what was going on, even though he lived in a different house. As soon as Hsiao-quai went into labour, Tuan was there at the window, watching the proceedings with curiosity and, perhaps, concern.

We called the baby Kai. As always, the first few hours are nerve-racking as you watch and wait to see whether the mother will care for the baby. Being in the nursery at this point helped to that end, as a lot of maternal behaviour is actually learnt rather than instinctive, so if a baby can see what is going on in there it can be a help. Hsiao-quai ate the placenta and cleaned up Kai. The signs were promising, but she seemed to be having a problem with feeding; she just could not grasp the fundamental mechanics of the process. I took to sleeping in the nursery in the hope that I might be able to encourage her. That is always a risk. The instinct of a new mother would be to tell me to get lost. But I was cool with Hsiao-quai. We had history and she was very accepting. It's a case of needs must and knowing your animals. She let me stay and I was truly honoured by that.

I stayed on the mattress by her side all night. Kai was trying to suckle and was nuzzling into his mum, but he didn't know how to get the milk. That was when I gently leant over and carefully pushed his head towards Hsiao-quai's teat. It was the start. I stayed in again the next night, but by the following morning they were doing very well. Quite literally, all they need sometimes is a helping hand.

We spent much of that year introducing various individuals into suitable groups and, with our numbers growing, it became an increasingly consuming part of the job. I like our bachelor boys, but it must be said that yobbo, testosterone-addled adults can be a pain too. A family evolves over generations but, of course, we were having to manufacture groups as animals came to Monkey World. It is hard to introduce an adult male into an established group as they would be perceived as a threat, so those chimps end up with the bachelor boys. I think of it as a bad boys' club.

Inevitably, I would find my mind drifting back to Alice. I thought about how Megan was getting on and how she had developed from a helpless child, suffering a febrile convulsion, into a young woman who knew exactly what she wanted. It was as if she was born with her life planned out, as if she knew what was going to happen on any given day. She had been in the sea cadets and then won a scholarship to go to Welbeck Defence College near Loughborough. In time she would also get her degree and, as I write this, she is doing boot camp somewhere in the North Sea. I'm very proud of her and happy she has a passion. Poor Alice never had that chance to find one and, while I am not one for wallowing in the past, it was a distressing and troubled time.

Events at the park didn't help raise my spirits either. This was certainly the case when I had to go down to a place in Swansea where a man was selling baby capuchin monkeys. The RSPCA got involved as they felt it cruel to take these animals from their mother at such a young age merely for profit. I am a very practical person, but sometimes it is easy to get depressed about the way man treats animals. I know people look at my life with a degree of envy, but it is not all sweetness and light – in fact, more often, it's the stench of dung and dark days.

Another crushing blow came on July 24, 2005 when Alberto died. It was a huge blow as we'd tried so hard with him and felt we were making stumbling steps of progress, but Alberto was never a success story. He was so old when we got him that all the bad things that had happened to him were already deeply ingrained. If you can't teach an old dog new tricks, then it is doubly hard with a chimp. I was doing the rounds that morning and the poor chap woke up dead. Mike Nathan came down to do a postmortem and thought it was heart-related. Once again, Alberto had shown no symptoms. Sympathy is in short supply in the wild, so Alberto had hidden his weakness.

A week later, Jess, one of the hand-reared chimps from Windsor, gave birth to Rodders, named in honour of the late, great Rodney, and the cycle of highs and lows continued. Ups and downs, life and death, hope and frustration, all thrown into a melting pot and left to boil over. A fortnight after that Cathy gave birth to Ash, but she lost interest after a while and so, with the mum in rejection mode, we had no option but to remove the baby.

Monkey World was now involved with projects all over the world. People tipped us off if they came across animals they thought might be victims, while our knowledge was useful to those who shared our drive and passion. One of those places was Vietnam, where the Dao Tien Endangered Primate Species Centre was still in the planning stage.

I went to Vietnam for the first time in January 2006 on a recce with Jim and Alison. It was an eye-opener. We went first to the outskirts of old Saigon and I noted in my diary that I went for a walk around the town while the grown-ups had a meeting. Then we went to a bear bile farm on a fact-finding mission. It was awful. Bears were kept in cramped cages so that the farmers could get at their abdomens and extract the bile to sell as a medicine. The bears lived awful lives and then, when they were deemed washed up and no longer ripe for milking, they were killed for their meat, gall bladders, fur and feet. There was a ramshackle zoo there too, which was a horrible place, but they actually welcomed tourists as a way of funding their operation. I grimaced as I looked at 40 or so bears lined up in dog kennels, waiting to be drained. I thought I needed some evidence and so grabbed a couple of bile containers.

"Jeez, Jeremy! What the hell are you doing?" Jim said through gritted teeth. "You're going to get us all shot."

"Don't worry," I said. "I'm legitimately purloining them. Anyway, the problem is not stealing, it's getting caught."

I was happy that our not-so-merry band of orangs was growing. Joly came to the park from Moscow Zoo and then, that July, RoRo had her baby out in the middle of the enclosure where she had built a nest. I stayed out with her overnight but, although she had cleaned up the baby, Dinda, she was not feeding her. I ran a heater into the enclosure and made a shelter for her, because she still refused to come inside. Jim and Alison scratched their heads and John Lewis came down. We pondered our possibilities. In the end we took decisive action and frogmarched RoRo back into the house where she was anaesthetised and Dinda was removed.

A few days later, we tried to get the two back together but, after a while, RoRo got annoyed with the baby. Clearly, it was not going to work.

I juggled this task with one of the more unusual duties I have had during my time at Monkey World. Koko, one of the stump-tailed macaques was, to put it mildly, overweight. In fact, she was so fat that the loose folds of fat were rubbing against each other and getting very painful. I had to go in every day and give her a bed bath, sitting her on my lap while I rubbed ointment into the flabby folds. Then I would dry her off and put some soothing cream on her. Obviously, she was on a diet to try to thin her down, but you cannot starve an animal. It was a long, slow process.

It had been a difficult period in my life, dominated by Alice. And there were also my feelings about the secret that I had kept hidden from everyone, even myself, for many years. I had decided I would come out of the closet, so to speak, on my 50th birthday. So one night shortly before, I went around to Jim and Alison's to reveal all. For years Jim had known I was harbouring some dark secret and he would always say that he was going to drag it out of me one day. So I sat him and Alison down. I took a deep breath. I had hoped my mother's death would bury these ghosts for me, but they hadn't. I felt the need to share it. And so I hurriedly told them that I had been sexually abused by my mother. It had become apparent to me only recently how truly scarred I had been by the matter.

As time had gone on, rather than the memories fading away, allowing me to move forward, the inner turmoil seemed to increase and perhaps even grow out of all proportion. I do not wish to dwell on this period in my life, but I feel a biography should be honest, warts and all, and while I am not one for raking over the past, there is no doubt that this abuse affected my behaviour, both at the time and since. The unmerited but unavoidable guilt I had been forced to live with ever since has always been lurking somewhere in the shadows.

Jim and Alison were a huge help and very sympathetic. Jim later told me that he thought the secret I was harbouring was that I had killed someone or something, and I was relieved to have told them. I am not into group analysis, sitting down and holding hands, but I have done an enormous amount of self-analysis. I don't know why it seemed the right time then to open up to others, but I was in between wives and it seemed to make sense. I was glad I did.

I wanted to be alone on my 50th birthday. There were a few reasons for this. One was that my kids had sprung a surprise 40th party on me a decade earlier and I did not want a repeat. "Which bit of me don't you know?" I asked them. It was also a milestone and I wanted to go on a round-the-coast-of-Britain bike ride to mark it. I needed to satisfy my wanderlust and I craved some solitude. More than anything, though, it provided me with the space for reflection, and I thought about my mother and what she did.

One of the horrible consequences of sexual abuse is that the victim often feels everything is his or her fault. I had wrestled with that but realised how things fell into place because of her actions – how she had made me live in the caravan, how she had cast me off. Of course, that had made me think that I was somehow to blame. I have no idea why my mother would have done what she did, but her warped view of life was shown when she received the money for selling Pan's Garden. My mother used that to buy her partner a Bentley, Pie a car, and Diana and Phoebe horses. I got half a bottle of lager.

A final, twisted facet to this story is that my mother later started a partnership with a man named Terry Mills. In 2008 Mills, a magistrate who visited primary schools to exhibit animals, was jailed for nine months for downloading child pornography. I cannot comprehend what goes on in the minds of these people, but it seemed a remarkable coincidence.

I had a vivid childhood memory of my mother spreading my grandfather's ashes on the North Yorkshire Moors and I felt drawn back there. I had already taken Diana there when our mother died. The others wanted to scatter her ashes with Baba. I told Diana I knew the exact spot and so I took her there to show her. I had no feelings for my mother but it made Diana feel good. Then, for some reason, I felt I wanted to be there on my 50th birthday.

I had decided to raise money for Julia's House, a local hospice for children with life-limiting conditions. I put a small sign up in the Monkey World shop window seeking sponsors. One who signed up was a huge balding biker who said he would give me some money, but also asked to see the bike I would be using on my journey. I showed him my Fazer.

"If you're going round Britain on that you'll need a

new seat," he said. "I do upholstery. Leave it to me."

That was my introduction to a gentle giant named Grant Surgey. He took away my seat and spent a month improving it. In the interim I tied a pillow on the seat and attracted some funny looks when I rode down to Poole Harbour for the weekly biker gatherings. I was relieved when Grant returned the seat and told me that it would be far more comfortable now.

"If you don't mind, could I ride round with you for a bit on the trip?" he asked.

"Of course," I replied.

I didn't plot a route but, after spending the night on Robin Dunham's boat in Brighton Marina, I picked up Grant and we set off.

There was no fanfare, but it was nice to be riding away from my troubles. Grant left me at the Dartford Tunnel and then I travelled alone through Suffolk and Norfolk, up through Lincolnshire and on to Whitby.

I had been fighting this bloody thing for years and I felt I was finally getting it off my back. I had no B&Bs booked, apart from one night in Whitby because I knew I wanted to visit Baba on the moors. Why? I don't know. I was riding around the coast of Britain and maybe I had skirted around the edge of my secret too. Now I had shared it with Jim and Alison and, in a way, it was halved. A week later I had ridden 3,000 miles. I had come a long way.

19

Jim

It was not long after that trip that I went to Jim and Alison's for dinner one night and suspected something was wrong with Jim. We had finished eating and conversation was drifting when Jim invited me to take a walk with him in the garden. It was totally out of character, but I thought little of it at the time and we wandered outside into the cold midwinter embrace and stood admiring his pond. It was not long before Jim started opening up.

"Do you know one thing I'm afraid of?" he began.

"What's that?" I replied, thinking Jim was about as fearless as anyone I had ever met.

"Being buried alive," he said. "Don't know why, but

I have this dread of being buried or cremated when I'm not actually dead."

I raised my eyebrows and sunk my hands deeper into my pockets, the cold providing a fitting backdrop to such morbid thoughts.

"I want you to promise something," Jim continued. And what followed was how I came to make my pact with Jim. By the time we went back inside and shut the door on the blackening sky, I had vowed that I would stay with him after he died. I had promised that I would do my best to ensure that there was no lid on his coffin and, most importantly, I had said I would check to make sure he really was dead before he went into the fiery furnace of the crematorium.

I came away that night with my mind dazed and confused. I remember wondering where on earth Jim's confession had come from and thinking that this was the heaviest conversation we had had in a quarter of a century of friendship. On that drive home, I asked myself a lot of questions and wondered why he had decided to give me this information and make this pact. Nevertheless, I could empathise because I remember Pie reading Edgar Allan Poe's *Tales of Mystery and Imagination* to me when I was a small child. Those stories were filled with death and plague and premature burials and I had been frightened out of my wits. Jim's words took me back to those breathless nights with Pie squeezing me through an emotional mangle. I got home and got on with life. I had made a promise to Jim and I would carry it out if fate put me in that position. Needless to say, I sincerely hoped it was a promise I would not have to keep.

It was not long afterwards that Jim took me into his confidence once again. We were at his house and he contrived to separate us from Alison.

"If I should die, Jeremy, I want Alison to move on," he said.

"Right," I said, dumbfounded.

"I want her to find someone else."

I was even more gobsmacked by this remark because, previously, Jim had always instructed me to kill any male who even dared to look at this lady with whom he was besotted. Now he was telling me he wanted her to find a new partner. It made little sense.

It was that December, in 2006, when Jim and Alison went on a trip to Australia. Opportunities over there were opening up for the world's greatest entrepreneur, so he headed off with due excitement. I stayed at home and carried on with my well-worn routine. I am a creature of habit and so I took the same route around the park every day, checking that all the chaps were okay, administering the contraceptive pills to those who were on the list, noting any problems and marinating myself in coffee. I did not give any great thought to Jim letting his guard down to me, and busied myself with caring for Amy and the rest. Knowing Jim, I suspect that if he felt there was a problem, he would have done what he always did and simply ignored it and hoped it would go away.

It was quite normal for Jim and Alison to depart to foreign climes and for the trips to be open-ended. Usually, they were rescuing some poor so-and-so from a life of cruelty or neglect, and it was hard to put exact time limits on those missions, as politics and due process were temperamental.

However, as the weeks passed by and a new year began, the grapevine throbbed with rumour and question. It was always the same: "When are they coming back?"

I struggled to satisfy everyone.

"I have no idea," I said truthfully, "but I am sure there is a perfectly good explanation."

But as time went on and no word came to explain their prolonged absence, the staff became increasingly concerned. The lack of communication I had with our adventuring duo was unusual, but I was determined to at least try to promote a sense of normality. It was not easy and the curiosity was mounting right up until January 10, 2007, when my telephone rang.

"Jeremy, it's Jim. How are things over there?"

"They're fine. Everything's okay. How are you?"

There was a slight pause before he delivered the sledgehammer. "Well, they're not good actually. I've been diagnosed with second-stage liver cancer." Another pause. "I don't want you to tell anyone, but I wanted to let you know."

"Christ!" I muttered.

"Jeremy," Jim intoned from halfway round the world. "I need you to step up to the situation."

"Of course," I replied.

It was not a long conversation, but it was one that altered everything. Jim was my oldest and dearest friend, my best mate, but I am a pragmatic person. I told him he knew where I was if he needed anyone to lean on or, indeed, if he needed to punch someone in the mouth. I focused on him telling me to step up to the situation. That became ingrained on my mind. It was a poignant request. Jim and Monkey World were depending on me.

There was no prognosis at the time, so the first thing

I did after replacing the receiver was to Google liver cancer. I also knew several people who had experience of cancer and I rang round to find out all I could. The horrible truth behind the words, both written and spoken, was liver cancer was a bad one.

Jim wanted to come back to Monkey World, to the dream he had created, but after an epic journey taking in Sydney, Cannes and Los Angeles, he and Alison ended up in New York. His health deteriorated rapidly and resulted in him going to the Cabrini Medical Center on East 19th Street, near Gramercy Park. Suddenly, I began to see pieces of an unformed jigsaw fitting into place. I remembered how Jim had stopped walking around the park as he usually did and had taken to using a golf buggy. I had never thought twice about it at the time, but now realised it was a reflection on his ailing health. The jagged pieces moved and slotted into position. I recalled our late-night talks about being buried alive and about Alison moving on. It became abundantly clear that poor old Jim had sensed that he had a serious problem.

As so often happens, fate then delivered a double-whammy. Ten days after Jim had rung with his horrible news, I had a call from my sister saying that my father had died. I was numbed by the news in the sense that I felt little. It sounds harsh, I know, but I had long felt let down by him. I had been disappointed that he had refused my invitations to come and visit Monkey World and then had been sickened when he had decided to side with Mary Chipperfield over Trudy. My grandmother had contacted me before he died, beseeching me to make it up with him, but I felt that to do so would be hypocritical. He had seen Kenyon once in his life and, for all our differences, I had no problem with him seeing his grandchildren whenever he wanted. But there was no contact. After the Mary Chipperfield case, I was relieved finally to have a reason to break this false sense of loyalty.

Nevertheless, it hit me hard. I was still haunted by my past and I did a lot of looking inward, thinking about where I had come from and the forks in the road I had faced. I kept my father's passing to myself as I did not want to burden Alison with that as she tended to Jim. Much later, when she discovered what had happened, she was touched that I had bottled it up inside.

Contact with Jim and Alison remained sporadic. Alison is a wonderfully practical person, but she had good days and bad days and then days when she was crashing. We knew it was a very aggressive form of liver cancer. On February 16, I wrote in my diary that Jim had an emergency operation to remove his colon. In March he began to slowly wake up. Where there's life there's hope – it gave us a glimmer of optimism. But we were clutching at straws.

Jim wanted to come back to tell the staff himself, but Alison rang and said he had slipped into a coma. We decided that we would have to tell the staff. I called a meeting. I was not relishing that task, but after work I called them all into the cafeteria. I stood up and cleared my throat.

"Now, I know there is a lot of speculation as to where Jim and Alison are," I began. I could feel their eyes fixed on me. "Well, the fact is there is an issue. Jim has liver cancer. The chances are he is not coming back." I saw the heads sink along with the hearts. Jim was our leader and a hugely popular man. I am sure some of the staff wondered whether we could survive if Jim didn't.

I also told them that I, too, would be flying out to New York. I was glad that Jez Hermer was there. We had got to know him when he was serving in the Royal Marines in Sierra Leone and he rescued a chimp called Harry. Unfortunately, politics got in the way and we could not get Harry out of Africa. He died soon after being moved to a rescue centre there. We had kept in touch with Jez in the intervening years and he had just come out of the Army to begin a new stage in his life. He was now helping Alison on the management side and, although we knew that he would not be around for ever, we also knew he was an able mind and had the right heart for this task.

Three days later, I flew out of Heathrow at 5am. Alison wanted me to be there and I will always do what a friend and boss asks. I arrived at 1.30pm and Jim was unconscious. I stayed at the hospital with Alison and her sister, Anne. Jim's family were from New York and so were regular visitors, but Alison kept a bedside vigil. Being the sort of person she is, she also managed to change all the hospital rules and regulations regarding visiting times. "I'm not going home," she said definitively. There was no point arguing.

The following day, I went to the hospital and spent the day with Jim. He was still unconscious. I persuaded Alison to come back for something to eat. Our minds were all rampaging thoughts and unspoken fears. Slowly, shafts of hope broke through the gloom. "Jim more responsive today," I wrote in my diary for March 11, but he remained unconscious. Back at the hotel, I rang Lee to make sure everything was fine at Monkey

World. He said it was, but I doubt he would have told me even if it wasn't.

We began to live in a limbo land of groundhog days and slow-dawning reality. I watched as Jim had dialysis treatment and then had a tracheotomy, an operation to insert a tube into his neck to facilitate his breathing. He was still unconscious, still unrecognisable from the vibrant figure who had first sucked me into his magnificent dream while holding court in the cafeteria at Howletts Zoo.

"Everyone thinks I'm mad," he had said.

"This isn't a job," he would say if people complained about the hours or money.

I hoped I was helping Alison. That was all I wanted to do. And we tried to get through to Jim. One thing that had always amused him was the way I could recite Rudyard Kipling's *Just So Stories* off by heart. He thought it was a great trick and I was happy to oblige him because I loved those animal tales. I sat in the anodyne room at the Cabrini Medical Center, the New York snow forming a white veil outside the window, and began to read again.

Them that takes cakes
Which the Parsee-man bakes

Makes dreadful mistakes.

It was a way of countering the bad days. Although he was very distant and barely conscious, you could sense if you were making contact with him. Alison spoke to the doctors and it was clear that the outlook was bleak.

"We could give him mild chemotherapy," the doctor explained.

She asked me what I thought. "What have we got to lose?" I said. "Look at him. What have we got to lose?"

Then he wanted to scratch, but that made it worse; and then he lay down on the sands and rolled and rolled and rolled, and every time he rolled the cake crumbs tickled him worse and worse and worse.

I was at the hospital on March 15 by 7.30am. There was some recognition from Jim that day but he was still obviously distressed. I wrote in my diary: "He had the controversial chemo today." It was controversial because you get to a point where it's kill or cure. There was no other option.

The following day the clouds broke and the snow

became a blizzard. It was unlike any snow I had seen at home, thick, relentless confetti silently wiping away all features. Cars became stranded and the manic noise of New York was softened by the drifts. Jim had dialysis in the morning and seemed to respond well. That night we took Alison out for a meal at an Italian restaurant. And the snow kept falling.

On March 17, I made a short entry in my diary: "Jim died at 4pm."

20

Dead End

I WAS HOLDING one of Jim's hands and Alison the other when Jim passed away. It was a chain of friendship. I cried. I had not shed tears for my mother or father but I did for Jim. It had definitely been a case of when rather than if, but that did not soften the blow. I had lost my best pal. I felt dreadful. I remembered how he had somehow given me the strength to carry on when he opened up to me as I lay in a semi-conscious state after my car crash a quarter of a century earlier, and felt wretched that I could not return the favour. Then, Jim had revived me and taken Amy to the vet. It was as if he had restorative powers. But despite by best efforts, my desire and my *Just So*

Stories, Jim just faded away.

There was nothing I could do now apart from honour his last request. I had reassured him that it would be possible because I had checked out the feasibility with a friend who worked back at Taylor's Garage and did funerals in his spare time. He had reasoned that it would be tricky to stay with Jim the whole time, but it was not impossible. Nothing was. As that had been Jim's mantra throughout this entire pipe dream, I felt ready to act.

Alison also knew all about Jim's paranoia and his last wish. She spoke to the surgeons and explained I was his right-hand man and had made a pact. She had lots of things to sort out and so we said our goodbyes and she left me to babysit Jim.

The undertaker arrived and I told him what I wanted to do. He was shell-shocked, but you score socially in the States with an English accent and we clicked. The undertaker was used to dealing with grieving people and so perhaps he was humouring me. Maybe he saw me as a mad English eccentric.

The snow had not let up for hours and rivers of white flowed between the huge black skyscrapers.

"There's one problem," he said.

"What's that?" I said, knowing in my heart that

there were far more than one.

"The bodies usually go out of the back of the hospital. Not so upsetting, you see. Only trouble is, with all the snow, I can't get the hearse around the back."

"So?"

"So we'll have to go out through the front door."

Jim would have loved the sight that followed. It was a scene straight out of *The Keystone Cops* as we wheeled him on a gurney through the corridors. Luckily, it was so late that they were not too busy, but there was a smattering of workmen fixing the electric doors, which had all broken down in the cold. Feeling a mixture of intense grief and exhilaration, I managed to wheel Jim out of the hospital and we got him in the hearse.

On the way, I ran through the whole story.

"He was scared of being buried alive," I told my new friend. "So I said I would stay with him until he was cremated and, just beforehand, check to make sure he really was dead."

The undertaker's puzzlement was palpable but he was happy to help. I told him how Jim did not want a lid on his coffin, but the undertaker shook his head.

"Can't do that," he said. "But I can leave the lid loose instead of screwing it down."

I reasoned Jim would have accepted that.

I left Jim in the bowels of the Chapel of Rest and went to his mother's house where we were staying. Then it was Monday. My big day.

I asked Alison if she was going to the crematorium. She wasn't because she was organising the actual church service which would take place the following day at a local Catholic church. My new undertaker pal had done his best to facilitate our clandestine undertaking because I am quite sure we were flouting every rule.

"I've booked him for the first cremation of the day," he told me. "It's a bit quieter then. Here's the plan."

With the air of someone out of a James Bond film, he then whispered the mechanics of our grand plan to grant Jim Cronin's final wish.

I could feel the heat from the furnace trying to burst through the red cloth. There was myself, the undertaker and the man from the crematorium in the room. The lid of Jim's coffin had been left loose as promised. Then, just as Jim was about to go into the fire, my new friend piped up with some excuse to take the man from the crematorium outside for a moment. This was my chance. The second they left the room, I lifted the lid of Jim's coffin and touched him on the nose and said, "I'll sithee". He was stone cold and I had seen and felt enough dead animals to know there was no coming back. Of course, I had known this already, but I had to satisfy Jim's request. In among all the feelings of sadness and gloom, I actually felt pleased that I had managed to pull it off by the time the duo returned.

It was early in the morning. I walked about the crematorium and the vast memorial gardens, which were as big as Monkey World. I looked at the tombstones, spread out from the building like petrified ripples. An ocean of grief. One of my great loves is to get lost. Literally. I enjoy the freedom that comes from losing your bearings. At home, that means I will occasionally take off on my motorbike and have no idea where I am riding. It's that sense of wanderlust again, that feeling I first encountered when standing on the North Yorkshire Moors and counting the stars with Scruffy, my faithful old English sheepdog. Now, I was in a part of a foreign city where I did not know a soul. It was the perfect place to walk and think. About the incredible journey that Jim, Alison and I had come on. I usually try to programme myself to think about where we are going rather than where we have been, but I grew increasingly reflective and remembered the struggles when we had first started, the things we did to survive, the trickery and the schemes.

We were at our lowest ebb and I shed more tears,

but as I looked back over our story, I could not help but think that dreams really do come true.

In this thoughtful mood, I kept walking and soon found myself outside the main gates of the crematorium. That was when I saw the sign. Even amid my darkest thoughts, I had to smile. Then the smile cracked into a laugh and I wished Jim had been there to see it. Across the road from the crematorium, directly opposite, at the entrance to a cul-de-sac was a large sign with big, bold capital letters declaring

DEAD END

The next day was the service at the Catholic church with family and friends. The man taking the service had been Jim's old priest and so he gave it a personal touch which was nice. Finally, we flew back to England. Alison got special permission to carry the ashes, and clutched them in her lap throughout the flight. I was glad that she was bringing him home.

There is nothing like living with animals to keep you focused. My father was right on that. Wallowing is a good thing and has its place, but there comes a point where you have to face the truth and get on with life. It was a relief to take my well-worn route around the park to check on everyone. There had been no great crises while we had been away. Sally went mad, screaming and rushing around, her delight at seeing me back obvious to all. Then I got to Amy's enclosure. It was good to see the old girl. She looked at me, utterly nonplussed, and went back to what she was doing as if to say, "I thought we'd got rid of you."

Strangely enough, I spent a lot of the time in the weeks after Jim's death with Jimmy, one of the original Spanish beach chimps who had developed a nasty infection on his leg. John came down to look at it and said we would have to amputate it if it got any worse. I should point out that these wounds were not any reflection on how we look after our animals. We give them the very best care, but the fact is this is how animals behave and you cannot control it. Chimps, in particular, get wounds all the time and someone bites a lump out of someone else on an almost daily basis.

I started going in with Jimmy and was nervous as hell. He was in one bedroom and I was in another. Slowly we raised the sliding door between us. We generally got on fine, but invading an animal's space is different. Think of it like having a colleague at work. You get on well enough in the office, but if he suddenly walked into your front room, turned over the TV and helped himself to your cocktail cabinet, you might be a bit miffed. It is a territorial thing. Luckily, Jimmy was just pleased to see me, but the adrenaline was pumping in those first few seconds when he had access to me.

Jimmy had deteriorated while I had been in New York, but I started bathing his wound with a disinfectant. Once Jimmy refrained from drinking the bowl of disinfectant, we began to make some progress. I didn't try to dress the wound because a chimp would discard the dressing straightaway. I also think fresh air is a good medium for healing. The only exception to that was Charlie. It was just another way in which he was special but even he gave it only two days before he took a dressing off his finger. Jimmy, meanwhile, had a long way to go, but slowly he recovered and then we had the pleasure of reintroducing him to his group.

Inevitably, the park had a different atmosphere without its leader. We were like a group of chimps, bereft of our dominant male and not knowing what to do. All we could do was survive. On April Fool's Day there was a summit meeting with Alison, John, who was also a trustee, Jez and me. It was a general rallying call. It didn't need saying but, in some way, it was good to have it out. The show would go on.

Several months passed and in June we had a memorial service for close friends and relatives. The response to his passing was comforting and both he and Alison would receive MBEs. Then, on June 24, we actually closed the park, something we almost never do. I might point out that the last Christmas Day I had off work was in 1973, although that is my own doing and I would not have it any other way. This was different, though, and special. It was Jim's memorial service for all our supporters.

My guitar teacher, John Wines, was there. He had put me in touch with a band, Midlife Crisis, and I joined them on stage for most of the second set. Alison held it together. It was a nice day but very sad. I would have done anything for Jim. We were single-minded people trying to get on with things. There had been good days and bad days, but plenty more of the former. I rattled a collection box and made £7,000.

I remember thinking how the instinct not to die is an amazing thing. It is what the animal world is based upon and it is also what fuelled Jim through the hardships of building Monkey World. We would not be beaten. And then, when you are, it is terrible. I cried for Jim, just as I had cried for Horace the tiger and Taffy the chimp.

Another guest at the memorial service was Graham

Mack, a DJ whom Jim loved for the way he did not care about what he said. He courted controversy, but was a good friend. Graham actually has a band and wrote a song called "Blues for Jim". The words sum up much of how I feel about a great man with a big mouth.

I really miss you, I miss your smiling face,
I really miss you, I miss your smiling face,
I never met anyone like you,
You made the world a better place.

I called you Jungle Jim, I loved to talk to you on the
air,
I called you Jungle Jim, I loved to talk to you on the
air,
You used to get me into trouble,
It was so much fun I didn't care.

You were smart like Joe Colombo, the best hustler
I'd ever seen,
You were smart like Joe Colombo, the best hustler
I'd ever seen,
And now you're not around,
We've got to carry on to fulfil your dream.

If you were here tonight, I wonder what you'd say,
If you were here tonight, I wonder what you'd say,
It'd mean a lot to me,
If you said I did okay.

I really miss you, I miss your smiling face,
I really miss you, I miss your smiling face,
There'll never be another,
You made the world a better place.

21
The 88

I SPEND AN inordinate amount of time with the unfortunate. That is the life I have chosen and, for all the
joy I get from being in close proximity to a myriad of
wonderful animals, I am never far from another horror
story. I have seen death and destruction on an almost
daily basis and it is sometimes hard to maintain a spirit
of optimism. That is why the story of David is so remarkable and a touchstone for hard times.

Jim called the stump-tailed macaques the ugly monkeys. "Ugly and proud," he would say. They had the
red faces of badly sunburnt holidaymakers and black-
rimmed eyes that made it look like they were wearing
mascara. In March 2001, David developed a serious

stomach problem that baffled medical science. I took him over to see Mike Nathan at his veterinary practice at Blandford, and, after an initial examination, Mike decided to do an exploratory operation. This entailed cutting David's stomach open from top to bottom and literally getting to the heart of the problem. It was not long before Mike was up to his elbows in blood and guts as he checked for blockages or ulcers or anything untoward. Anyone considering a career in this line might want to note that it is most definitely not for the squeamish.

It is often the case that mere manipulation improves a problem and so, with nothing major found, Mike began bundling David's guts back inside him. Then he took out a needle and began to sew him up. That was when it happened. The buzz and beep of the monitors went into overdrive and formed the backbeat to David's demise.

"I'm losing him," Mike said. He checked the chest. "There's no heartbeat." I had been in enough operating rooms to know the tell-tale signs and realised we were fighting a lost cause. No heartbeat, no pupil reaction. It was another horrible day at the office.

After well over two minutes without a heartbeat, we began to disconnect poor old David from all the monitors. Mike then picked up his needle again and was about to put in a couple of butterfly stitches, just to keep his insides where they were meant to be, before we set about the grim task of disposing of the cadaver. As I turned my back, I heard Mike almost whisper, "I don't believe it." I twisted around. "He's breathing."

Mike proceeded to stitch him up properly, for life rather than death, and I took David back to the park. That night I went to see him at 10 o'clock and gave him his routine jab. He was fine. He still is. In a job where you are taxed by a catalogue of heartache, it was the most heart-warming of moments.

Fast-forward six years and the hope that there might be life after death was something we were all clinging to. Losing Jim was a blow we never expected. Nothing could have prepared us for a loss of that magnitude and I can't honestly ever imagine fully recovering from his absence. I truly don't want to.

There were more losses as well. They say things come in threes and after Jim there was Grant. The big-hearted biker who had been so kind to me on my round-Britain trek was killed in a motorcycle accident. He was not a close friend, but his death shook me up. His generosity had touched me and his death made a big impact. I went to his funeral, where Grant's wish of there being no black was observed – no easy task for a funeral cortege of bikers. Grant had a pink coffin and there was a red Ferrari. I went on my new Harley and was painfully conscious that I was surrounded by proper bikers. I hoped I didn't fall over or make a fool of myself as we snaked along the roads towards the crematorium near Gatwick.

Then we lost Aris, the little orang who had come to us from Germany. He developed a nasty infection on his knee. I took him to see Mike and had it flushed out, but it did not go well and we ended up losing the little fellow on December 5.

Despite these awful events, I was on a high after starting a relationship with Lou, who had joined the park as our communications chief, helping to spread the word of our work and dealing with the increasing number of media inquiries. There was also a new unifying focus for everyone at the park – Alison, Lou, myself and all the other keepers – in the wake of Jim's death. Armed with my knowledge of Jim's passion for South American monkeys and his typically American attitude that everything relating to him should be bigger and better, we embarked on the largest primate rescue in history. It would be a living tribute.

Jim and Alison had been discussing the rescue well

before his cancer was diagnosed. Officials from a science laboratory at a university in Santiago, Chile had made contact with us. They had used a huge number of capuchins, the original organ-grinder's monkey, for invasive medical tests. Now they were under intense pressure from animal rights protesters. Staff there had been receiving death threats and they were desperate to offload them. You might say they wanted the monkeys off their backs.

It was a fresh morning when Alison called a meeting of the primate care staff in the canteen. She explained the situation in Chile and wanted to know whether we could take all of the capuchins. It was a one-time offer from the lab and she was concerned that some of them could be psychotic. The spirit of Monkey World, as originated by Jim, had always been "yes we can", so I nodded and said, "That's okay."

Others in the group voiced their agreement. In for a penny in for a pound.

"It's what Jim would have wanted," I added.

"I hope you know what you are letting yourself in for," someone piped up.

"Don't care," I responded. We generally waste little time on making decisions here at Monkey World, which is a policy that has worked just fine for me in two decades. And so that was how we committed ourselves to making history.

That August, just four months after Jim had died, word came through that we had got planning permission to replace one of the old enclosures with a shiny new timber-framed capuchin house. "The monkeys in Chile are now surplus to requirements and will either be retired or destroyed," Alison told the local paper. It had already become a labour of love, and the fact that Jim had a fascination with cappies, having encountered them when growing up on the streets of New York, made it a fitting challenge.

Stumbling blocks littered the path to Santiago. For a start, most commercial airlines were only interested in Santiago because of its lucrative role in transporting seasonal fruit. We quickly came to realise that fruit mattered more than monkeys and, with planes full of goods, there was no charity for our furry friends. The fact was that 88 boxed monkeys would leave no room for any other luggage or cargo.

In the end it was the Chilean air force that filled the role of saviour by putting a Hercules transport plane at our disposal, and on January 19, 2008, Alison and I began the first leg of our epic adventure by flying to Santiago via Madrid.

I now had a week to spend as much time as I could with the chaps and make as many notes and observations as possible. These would prove vital for when we returned home and attempted the hugely ambitious task of introducing these monkeys into large social groups.

Joining us soon after our arrival were the team from the TV series, Natalie, Geraint and Richard, who wanted to capture the rescue on film for the programme and posterity. Alison, meanwhile, became embroiled in the usual red tape that inevitably reared its head at the most inconvenient times. Usually Alison and Sue, our long-suffering office manager back at Monkey World, dealt with such matters in a two-pronged approach. That suited me because it left me to hang out with the chaps. When I first stepped into their dungeon-like rooms, I was staggered. Row after row of anxious faces stared back at me from steel cages. I realised most of them had not seen daylight for years and they had been locked away as afterthoughts. I stayed with them, chatted away and fed them through the bars. It was a humbling experience, but I should add that I was pleased to find that the cappies were remarkably stable people with few hang-ups, which was a tribute to the excellent care staff in the lab. These were mainly local folk employed to cater for the animals' basic needs and, whatever you might think about the morals of science, these particular people had done their job well.

That made little difference to the animal rights protesters who were encamped outside the university and had been waging a long-running battle against the academics. My stance, and that of Monkey World, is never to take sides in these matters and avoid being dragged into either protest or debate. My job was, purely and simply, to make sure the chaps were okay before we provided a sanctuary for them. Politics have never interested me. My only concessions to that field are being a communist for three weeks when I was a teenager and a long-standing ambition to have a Che Guevara tattoo.

The protests were vociferous and we realised that nobody would have any idea about our role in this ongoing saga. As far as they were concerned, they were right and the people inside were wrong. They did not differentiate between me and the researchers. To them, I was just another evil scientist and it was hard to ignore the placards, the megaphone and the images daubed on walls in red paint. It was not a place for neutrals, so we entered the lab via a rear door to avoid drawing attention to our secret mission.

Surveying the chaps one by one, cage after cage, I noted that the elderly dominant male, Grillon, was in some pain. Further examination showed that he was actually suffering with a tooth. A dentist was quickly called, Grillon was tranquillised and the tooth was expertly filled. Everybody else looked in good shape. I was sure we could at least try to move all 88.

There was an obvious urgency in the lab. The scientists wanted to see the back of their monkeys and were growing increasingly fearful of attacks from the protesters. The messages on the banners and the abuse hurled at the staff bridged the language barrier. It was a well-intentioned act of defiance but could easily have reached a tipping point. I just wanted us to get home safe and sound.

"They know something's going on," Alison told me as I emerged from the gloom of the dungeons with my pad of expanding notes.

"Who do?"

"The protesters," she said. "The sooner we get out of here the better."

The fact that the protesters had got wind of what we were up to convinced us that the safest course of action would be to load the cages onto the trucks in the dead of night. We gathered together at 9pm on January 25 and started work. Moving the cappies was not as difficult as you might imagine. Their sorry lives as experimental specimens meant they were used to being shepherded around in boxes, so we managed to get them into our own crates without too many emergencies. By 5am all 88 animals were safely crated and stashed in the back of the trucks that were winding their way to the airfield. I sat in the front of one and my heart pounded. I had visions of the protesters charging after us and the flicker of any headlight on the road induced a nervousness that I could not shake. Those nerves frayed further when I saw the Hercules transporter plane on the airfield. It was clearly an antique with four old propellers and, while it seemed in good condition, its vintage did little to ease my anxiety.

The air crew were utterly professional. We had met them back at the university, where they had measured the crates and done complex sums to guarantee they could fit all 88 into the hold and ensure all were accessible for checks and water. I looked across the runway to the park and hoped that the protesters would not make some last-ditch move to scupper our rescue.

"Okay, that's it. They're all in."

I looked at my watch: 6.30am. The propellers sparked into life and we took our seats. The Hercules rolled back the years and down the runway with a rumble. Then we were airborne. There was no turning back now.

We were a motley crew. There was Alison, myself and three lab vets who were coming with us. In addition, Geraint and Richard, our cameraman and soundman, were beavering away, getting shots of everything. I could not help thinking that this would make good TV.

As soon as we were up, we unstrapped ourselves from our flimsy collapsible seats, akin to deck chairs, and went to check on our travelling companions. It was a gruelling voyage for all of us. After two hours, we landed in north-east Brazil to refuel and then we made the long transatlantic trip to our next destination, Las Palmas. By now, body clocks were out of synch and alarm bells were ringing. The day passed in a blur.

I was jolted from my semi-wakefulness by a patch of turbulent air. One of the towers of crates lurched dangerously. The top box leant over and was in danger of crashing to the floor. The vets and I were on our feet when a trio of Chilean airmen rushed past us. They deftly secured the crates and quickly faded away again, like genies into a bottle.

Geraint and Richard then decided eating might help

fend off the chronic fatigue. It seemed a good idea. They unpacked a picnic they had stashed prior to take-off, complete with a bottle of wine. It was a surreal sight, but it seemed a good place to have a toast. Alas, it was not to be. Another flash and the three Chilean airmen appeared, shouting noisily and pointing at the wine. For a moment, I thought that we were going to be thrown off the plane, or at the very least court-martialled. Geraint sensibly stuck the wine back in his bag. That seemed to placate the genies, who once again faded whence they had come, back into the bottle.

Capuchins are one of the most intelligent and inquisitive species of monkeys, so they must have been amazed at the events of the previous 24 hours. Our 88 travelling companions had spent their lives confined in a science lab without even a window to the outside world, and now they were dodging protesters and boarding planes.

When we touched down in Gran Canaria, I was relieved to find they were in good condition. Strangely, despite their day jobs, they were healthier than some of the capuchins I had come across in the UK. One of these was Gismo, who was bred and sold for the UK pet trade and ended up living in a garden shed in Ipswich. His solitary confinement had made him an aggressive, angry soul and his owners had not been able to open his cage to clean it for fear of being bitten. Hence, he lived in urine-infested squalor. With his physical condition informing his mental one, he began picking at his own body, opening horrible sores and wounds, to the extent that he had amputated three inches of his own tail by the time we got to him. I am glad to say that the animals on the Hercules were in far ruder health than poor old Gismo.

It was now 6am. The morning after the night before. I had no idea what time zone I was in and was working only via night and day, dark and light. The air crew had now run out of flying hours and so, by law, were obliged to take a day off before completing the final leg. They parked the Hercules in some shade and I made sure there was plenty of food and water for the day ahead.

"I think we'd be better off at home," Alison said. Neither of us were the sort of people to be content with clicking out heels.

"There's a lot to do," I agreed.

"Why don't we fly back and make sure everything's ready. The cappies will be fine."

It was sorted. The Chilean ladies stayed with the cappies while Alison, Richard, Geraint and I travelled home via Madrid, although we lost Geraint on the way. A ticket mix-up in Madrid meant he had to stay in Spain and then make a mad dash home in time to film the arrival of the Hercules. So we three survivors limped into Monkey World late on January 27 in a semi-conscious and incredibly smelly condition.

I grabbed a few hours' sleep, but my mind was a frenzy of activity even if my body was shutting down. I woke to the familiar sound of the chimps. I dressed quickly and dashed out into the cold. I made a quick circuit of the park, checking on everyone and making sure they were all okay. Sally indulged in her usual mad greeting. Butch and the hooligans grinned and went back to their posturing. The orangs were all out of their bedrooms, except one. I didn't really need to ask who was causing the trouble. It was the reluctant ape. The contrary rarity.

"Hello, Amy," I said.

She huffed her approval. And stayed put.

I hastened to the new capuchin enclosure and was mightily relieved to see what a good job had been done in my absence. As always with these things, timing runs amok and things rarely happen in an orderly, stress-free manner. This time it looked like we were ahead of the game. I felt like Del Boy in *Only Fools and Horses* when he turns to Rodney and says, "I'm winning. I'm finally winning."

Somehow Alison had pulled off another miracle by getting quarantine status for Bournemouth Airport. We went there on January 29. There was no end of practical considerations to think about and Alison and I busied ourselves with those. The unspoken subtext was Jim. Monkey World was his baby and together we had spawned a beautiful monster. And this was *the* rescue. As I scanned the sky, I could not help drifting back to the first day we opened, when the punters had groused about the agoraphobic monkeys, and I had turned to Amy to save the day. I had saved her and she had saved me. Now we were saving 88 capuchin monkeys. We were making history. I am not a sentimental or religious man, but I felt that somehow, somewhere, Jim was cracking open a big smile at our sheer audacity.

I was urged out of my reverie by Alison crying, "There it is!"

High up above Bournemouth, I saw a black dot that grew with an attendant buzzing. We stood in silence as the Hercules tipped its wings and the outline of the plane took shape above us. Soon after, the Chilean air force were stood to attention by the side of the landed vessel as 88 capuchin monkeys were counted out and loaded into the back of the waiting trucks. It had been a rip-roaring success started by Jim and completed in his honour. The bottle of wine? We gave it to the air crew.

22

The New Generation

IT WAS NOT long after we got back that I noticed Amy had pregnancy swellings again. Maybe this time would be better. It seemed an awfully long time since I had hand-reared this furball and now I was dealing with a new generation. Ben and Pip were moving on and went in with Hananya's group. I felt the mantle of leadership had been thrust on Hananya too soon, but hoped the duo would find their feet.

And life carried on its rollercoaster route of highs and lows. Poor old Trudy, the chimp at the centre of the Mary Chipperfield storm, had lots of problems with her back, and we eventually ended up getting a huge, space-age scanner shipped in on an articulated lorry. The sight of little Trudy going into the oven, as I phrased it, was unforgettable. The scan showed numerous issues, but we continued to do our best for her. Sadly, her background meant she would never be able to recover completely, but we gave her anti-inflammatories and she has done pretty well since. That's life. It is a series of peaks and troughs.

That August I decided to take Lou to the Bulldog Bash near Stratford. This motorcycle convention is a huge affair, with people coming from all over Europe. I promised Lou it would be a treat and we got there early to ensure we got a good pitch for the tent. Unfortunately, a bunch of very noisy Welshmen decided to make camp next door to us and then proceeded to stay up all night. I put my head down on my clothes, which I was using as a pillow, and tried in vain to get some rest. Then came the rain and, as I'd made the mistake of pitching on a slope, we woke to find all Lou's clothes floating in a sea of mud. We baled out soon afterwards and went to stay with my friend, Colin, in Derbyshire, Lou vowing never to go camping with me again.

She left Monkey World soon after, although the two events were unrelated. Lou took a job as the senior publicity officer for Butterfly Conservation, based in Lulworth. It is a very worthy organisation and her job means she gets to hobnob with the likes of David Attenborough and Alan Titchmarsh. I was very pleased for her. We also got married, on September 6, 2008 and went to St Lucia for our honeymoon. Finally, after four previous attempts, I was convinced I had got it right. I still work seven days a week but I go on holiday now too.

My other woman, Amy, had more problems as she struggled with motherhood. Her baby was born in October but died. There was something about Amy that just seemed to make her unsuited to the role.

Nevertheless, I felt contented as I made my daily journeys on my quad bike, down the farm trails to work.

Megan was forging on with her career. Kenyon was a hippie doing carpentry. Jamie's hormones took him to live in Hull, reportedly the least desirable place to live in Britain. They are all different, as are all the animals I have worked with over the years. I never try to label people or apes.

The mornings here are generally quite peaceful. The air is chill and the apes and monkeys are all in their houses. It is the calm before the storm. I like watching them wake up. I see Paddy playing with the babies and it gives me a nice feeling. Then I see the others waking up, scratching, yawning and farting. There is not usually much noise at that time unless someone has been caught in bed with the wrong woman or suchlike. I give Sally's group their breakfast and that's the thing that sharpens the minds of the others. "Hey, why are they first?"

I feel blessed to share their lives and am grateful for the chance. It is why I feel slightly guilty about my minor celebrity status. There is even a Facebook campaign to get me knighted. Not long after the TV series started, I went down to Brighton Marina to see my friend, Robin Dunham, on his boat, and was bemused when people started coming up to me. I stopped at a little transport café on the way back and the waitress nearly dropped her pencil.

"You're that Jeremy from Monkey World, aren't you?" she screeched.

I just enjoy what I do. I'm indulging myself and work seven days a week because I want to. Nobody makes me work so many days that, if I added them all up, I'd have actually accrued four years off. This is my love and, like Jim said, it's more than a job. I'm not a TV star. I don't aspire to be Tom Cruise or even David Attenborough. I'm just a very lucky man.

That is not to say it has been an easy life: the emotional trauma can be severe, and it certainly was in January 2009 when I noted in my diary that Charlie was ill.

Dear old Charlie had been a lost soul for a while and kept separating himself off from the bachelor boys. I wanted to cheer him up, so when they were outside, I'd go into the pavilion with him and hang out.

He deteriorated fast after I first noted his illness. Charlie lost a lot of weight and was apathetic and listless, lying in his bed and barely responding to my words. At one point we had to put him on a drip, and while it was dreadful, there was also a sense of the inevitable. It's true that where there's life there's hope, but it seemed that Charlie was drifting towards an inescapable conclusion. It was like waiting for God. We had run out of options and on February 8 he passed away.

Charlie was iconic for us and it is fitting that we now have a magnificent bust of him and Jim together in the park. Every day on my rounds I stop by, touch Jim on the nose and thank these two for creating Jurassic Park and leaving the rest of us to look after the place. "I'll sithee," I say to Jim before moving on.

Two years to the day after Jim had passed away in New York, Pip died. Pip had also been born on Jim's birthday. I did the maths and worked out that the odds on that happening were one in 133,225. Pip had got a wound on the side of her leg and, although she would have survived without being sewn up, we felt it was the best option. Unfortunately, Pip died under anaesthetic. That was hard to take and a reminder of how dangerous anaesthetic can be.

Ben was still having problems too. Some people are obsessed with having mixed sex groups, but my theory is that it is not worth leading an unhappy, suppressed life for the sake of a five-second orgasm. Ben had been tried with other groups first but he found his true home only when he went in with the bachelor boys. They ruffled his hair and loved him, from big, bold Butch to Sammy throwing rocks as his welcome present. Ben had the time of his life in the bad boys' club.

There was a squirrel monkey to collect from a dilapidated farm in Sussex, and two capuchins from an ex-pat couple in Tarragona. There was much to do at Monkey World and much to do in Vietnam, where I went to help put electric fencing across the raging Dong-Nai river. It is a never-ending story.

Then, in November 2009, Hsiao-quai gave birth to a new baby. He was called Jin which means "handsome" in Chinese. As before, Hsiao-quai proved to be a good mother. The father was Gordon, which not only meant we had Gordon's Jin on site, but also gave Amy grandmother status. I may not be trying to save a species, merely to give these wonderful creatures a happy and contented life, but I felt a thrill of satisfaction at having kept Amy alive all those years ago and helped give rise to a new generation of orange people.

I was glad she was no longer a pet. In fact, many people are surprised when I tell them I don't like having pets. Animals are not meant to be domesticated in my view. I do have Pom Pom, the rescued dog, and Ted the cat, plus assorted chickens, but that's down to Lou. I prefer my animals wild. That was why I had to let Amy go. She had lived with me for years and would always have a special place in my heart, but it was not where she belonged.

It has been a great ride. From Pan's Garden and the house of horrors to a millionaire's estate and things money can't buy. I have met wonderful people like Jim and Alison and Lou, and beloved animals like Horace and Sally and Tuan. I don't know what the future is for orangs but I am glad that there are people out there working hard to help them. I think the odds are stacked against them, but to let these animals die out would be an incredibly selfish act on our part. If I have done my bit in a very small way, then I am happy. It is a two-way street. I may have helped to save orang-utans like Amy but, in return, I have been rescued by her and the orange people.

CAST OF CHARACTERS

Alberto

Male chimpanzee, rescued as an adult, who found it hard to integrate into a social chimp's everyday routine. His time at Monkey World was sadly short; he died of natural causes.

A-Mei

Female orang-utan rehomed from Pingtung Rescue Centre in Taiwan. With a reputation for being "spiteful" that she has never lived up to, A-mei is now the boss of our orang-utan nursery and is worth her weight in gold for performing her duties so well.

Amy

Female orang-utan with ATTITUDE... 99% of it bad! After a very shaky start in life with a poor prognosis, Amy developed into a very healthy – I hesitate to use this word – lady. I'm sure that living in such close proximity to me, with no orang influence for the first four years of her life, had an influence on her stoic attitude and her general holier-than-thou, deeply pessimistic manner. As she is a carbon copy of her mother, Jane, maybe it isn't all my fault? I have often stated, "Of all the orangs in all the world, why did I end up with this one?" I suppose I wouldn't have it any other way.

Aris

Young male orang-utan. Probably not a Mensa candidate,

but nevertheless a happy soul whose life at Monkey World was tragically cut short.

Banghi
Male orang-utan whose life was marred by constant bad health and being introduced to our electric fence by Amy, but who remained a nice fellow nevertheless.

Ben
Male chimp and Peggy's son, Ben was bottle-reared by me after Peggy neglected him. A very happy young man, his early life was spent with Pip up until her untimely death. Failing to be accepted by Hananya in his group, Ben has found true content-ment in Monkey World's bachelor, aka hooligan, group.

Beth
Among the first chimpanzees here in the park, Beth has a very well-established role in Paddy's group. She has lost practically half of one foot, including all but the big toe, which we believe was a result of her brutal capture from the wild in Africa.

Bobo
Adult female orang-utan and Kumang's mum. She arrived at Gordon Mills's after Belle Vue Zoo closed down. A perfect mother who also gave birth to Rosie but sadly died when Ku-mang was only 18 months old.

Bryan
A chimpanzee who came to Monkey World in 2006 with ter-rible problems after having his teeth knocked out by a pho-tographer.

Busta

As one of Paddy's deputies, Busta has an important role and takes his duties very seriously. The cause of his early bad temper and moodiness was identified as a bad tooth issue. A visit from super-vet, John Lewis, resolved this, and although never the life and soul of the party, Busta is now a far mellower chap.

Butch

Arriving at Monkey World as a companion of Charlie from Spain, Butch has always been a survivor. A very tough individual, he is now the leader of the bachelor group, which, as you might imagine, is not a job for the faint-hearted.

Carli

Former film and TV star, Carli was bred for the acting industry and came to Monkey World when his last owners realised he needed to live as a chimp.

Charlie

Greatly missed male chimpanzee of exceptional good nature and trusting disposition, despite having suffered probably the worst physical, mental and drug abuse of any animal we have rescued.

Chatta

Chatta arrived as a lone individual from Spain where she had worked as a photographer's prop. As a youngster she served her quarantine period in my home and soon proved to be a very independent and tough young lady.

Cherokee

Spoilt, hand-reared pet puma from the Pan's Garden era. Famously escaped one day, leading to farcical and violent scenes.

Chico

A Monkey World chimpanzee, now sadly deceased, with a large build to match the size of his heart. A very fair group leader.

Cindy

A member of Monkey World's first chimpanzee clan, Cindy has always been Paddy's lady.

Clin

One of our second Spanish shipment, I christened her after my father as, like him, she had only one eye and the same selfish attitude. The first chimp birth in the park was Clin's ill-fated daughter, Simone.

Coco

Adult male orang-utan of extremely low intellect, which he made up for by being a nice chap (even though he once beat me up during my time at Little Rhondda).

Digger

Male dingo from Pan's Garden with the ability to be reasonably tame with humans, while retaining some natural, wild behaviour, as my father found out to his cost.

Ermentrude

Typically good-natured, female Indian rock python.

Flossy
Elderly female gorilla, a caricature of everyone's favourite granny, sold to Longleat to make way for the orange people at Little Rhondda.

Fred
Baby patas monkey in need of a mum. My schoolboy pet.

Gordon
Our first successful orang-utan to be born at Monkey World, Gordon was bottle-reared by Mike Colbourne. Gordon has evolved his own group comprising two ladies, Hsiao-lan and Hsiao-quai, along with Tuan and Hsiao-quai's son, Kai, and last but not least, Gordon and Hsiao-quai's son, Jin.

Gunga Din
Male ring-tailed lemur with homicidal tendencies.

Guy
Young adult male orang-utan whose priorities, like many of his species', were food and a good woman. My first introduction to the orange people at Colchester Zoo.

Hananya
Male chimp smuggled into Israel for the illegal pet trade, he is now a benevolent group leader at Monkey World.

Harry
Adult male orang-utan whose priorities again were food and sex, he arrived at Gordon Mill'ss menagerie with an unfortunate, but unfair, reputation.

Horace

Tiger who had a huge impact on my life during his own solitary life on Gordon Mills's estate.

Hsiao-quai

A refugee orang-utan from Taiwan, Hsiao-quai is our example of mothering perfection, rearing both Kai and Jin. Maybe a daughter next time will put the icing on the cake.

Jambi

Baby orang-utan who died young and never really had the chance to develop a personality at Little Rhondda. Jane's daughter.

James

Male orang-utan with whom I only had a brief time but who seemed very contented, despite the vagaries of the Anthropoid Ape Advisory Panel.

Jane

Read Amy's profile as Jane is clearly Amy's mum! Jane continues to thrive in her Californian home at the San Diego Zoo. Born around 1960, she is about 50 years old now, which is ancient for an orang, but I am pleased to report that her stroppy attitude hasn't mellowed with age.

Jimmy

Chimp Jimmy was one of Paddy's deputies at Monkey World before his anti-social behaviour secured a home for him in the bachelor group. Jimmy needed intensive nursing when he developed a serious infection in a leg wound, but now enjoys a reasonable rank in his current group.

Johni
A female chimpanzee, she is Clin's daughter and was bottle-reared by me after Clin failed in her maternal duties. Johni is a very tough young lady who has a high social standing in Hananya's young tribe. Named after John Lewis, the vet, who was responsible for Clin's contraception!

Joly
Female orang-utan, Joly is a hand-reared refugee from Moscow Zoo where she was rejected by her mother. Joly came to live with us at Monkey World because we are the official crèche for orphaned orang-utans. Mike Colbourne travelled to Moscow to escort her home. Joly lives with A-mei, an adult lady from Taiwan and an ideal foster mum, in our orang nursery.

Kai
Male orang-utan and son of Hsiao-quai, our excellent orange mother person. Comfortable to share his mum with recently arrived half-brother Jin. An important member of Gordon's family.

Kareen
Female brown bear from my time in Pan's Garden. A good-natured, sociable and contented lady.

Katie
Small, very sociable female gorilla on the Millses' estate, who enjoyed both human and gorilla company.

Kumang

Young female orang-utan who knew exactly what she wanted after being left motherless at 18 months. Bobo's daughter.

Kylo

A chimpanzee from Spain, Kyko has ended up in Monkey World's bachelor group as a low-ranking individual. This position leaves him free to have loads of fun with the sub-group of adolescent rebels.

Lady

Tiger cub – and sister of Horace – who was reared at Little Rhondda together with her other brother Peter.

Louis

Adult male orang and Amy's dad. Extremely intelligent but physically very small and possessor of little-man syndrome.

Lucky

Arriving at Monkey World via the Pingtung Rescue Centre, Lucky remains an independent young lady with a strong personality. She is one of Tuan's favourites and enjoys that status.

Lulu

One-armed female chimp born in a travelling circus and one of the most distinctive figures at Monkey World.

Memba

Proud ladies' man of a gorilla, bought by Gordon Mills from a Dutch dealer, who has since lived up to this image as a prime breeder in San Diego Zoo.

Mojo

A chimpanzee from Spain, Mojo has always been an aloof and self-contained character, never appearing to need the close company of either his own species or humans. Mojo sported a distinctive bandit mask pigment on his face as a youngster, but sadly this feature has faded.

Mona

Female chimp who suffered a similar amount of human abuse to dear old Charlie, prior to spending a few happy years with us here at Monkey World.

Monty

Male gorilla who was very aloof and anti-social – possibly as a result of being mistaken for a female when bought from a Dutch dealer by Gordon Mills.

Ollie

Gordon Mills's adult male gorilla, afflicted by a combination of little-man syndrome, a small brain and few friends.

Pablo

Adult male chimp, formerly with a Spanish circus, who joined the "fun" at Pan's Garden. With advanced social skills and a charming nature, he was also responsible for one of my first animal-inflicted injuries when I was still a toddler.

Paddy

Adult male chimpanzee and the undisputed leader of Monkey World's first group. A private individual, he is the ideal leader for a harmonious (hard to believe with chimps!) ape family.

Peggy

Another Spanish refugee chimp, Peggy has always been a tough lady. Named after the late Peggy Templer, she is Ben's mum, although she chose not to look after her son. Peggy is now one of the dominant ladies in Hananya's tribe.

Peter

Tiger cub, brother of Horace, reared at Little Rhondda together with their sister, Lady.

Pip

A young female chimpanzee who tragically died after an operation. Born at Monkey World, she was a successful and sociable group animal after being hand-reared, along with Arfur, by me in my home. Pip's mum was Cherri. Never quite sure who Pip's dad was in that multi-male group.

Pongo

Baby male orang-utan and son of Daisy, who developed into a really likeable chap in his sadly short life at Little Rhondda. He suffered from polycystic fibrous dysplasia and lived only six months, The poor chap was one in a million.

Prissy

Young adult female orang-utan at Colchester Zoo who was happy with a little food and a good man to feel put upon by.

Rhanee

A particularly smart and sociable female Bengal tiger, Rhanee was Horace's mum.

Rimba

Baby orang-utan who never really had the chance to develop a personality before her premature death. Jane's daughter.

Rocky

A chimpanzee from Spain where he was given Valium to calm him, Rocky remains a tough little fellow who enjoys his life in Monkey World's bachelor group and makes friends easily.

Rodney

One of the chimp exiles from the failed Windsor Safari Park, Rodney was the dominant male of that dysfunctional group. He enjoyed being boss of a more relaxed family at Monkey World until a surprise take-over bid by Hananya. He died soon afterwards.

Rooty

Male wild swine of high intelligence who appeared to enjoy every activity before his tragic demise when Pan's Garden closed.

RoRo

An adult female orang-utan from Pingtung Rescue Centre. RoRo is a perfect example of her species, except for her failure to rear either of her daughters, Hsiao-ning and Dinda, leaving this to our human nanny, Mike Colbourne. Should Tuan ever credit us with an opinion, I believe he would say that RoRo is his Number One lady.

Sally

A female chimpanzee whose failure as a sociable animal was

turned into a success story when we set her up as Monkey World's foster mother. Unable to be dominated, Sally chooses the youngsters she will mother, and has a marked preference for male babies. She also has a particular affection for me, so we work well together in caring for the younger chimps. She has developed a friendship with Lulu, who is a fiercely independent lady and, hence, poses no threat to Sally.

Sammy
One of the original chimpanzee arrivals at Monkey World, Sammy relies on his good nature to win both human and chimp friends. As an animal of little brain, Sammy is one of the easy-going members of the bachelor group, but he is a big lad and not to be crossed.

Scruffy
Male old English sheepdog of very little brain but vast amounts of bonhomie and forgiveness. My companion during my six-month hiatus after leaving home.

Seamus
Cherri's first child, Seamus was bottled-reared by me after being ignored by his mum. Seamus's nature made him an ideal candidate for the bachelor group where he enjoys a very happy life with the boys.

Shere Kahn
A typically aloof male Bengal tiger. Horace's dad.

Taffy
One of the original group of chimpanzees from Spain, Taffy was

a very hard character who won few friends. His early demise from pneumonia was the first ape death at Monkey World and had a major impact on me.

Tessy
Adult female gorilla from the Gordon Mills era who clearly had delusions of grandeur.

Toto
A massive African bull elephant tusker who lived in a herd at Howletts Zoo in the mid-1980s and became a very close neighbour of mine. His fall in his enclosure one Boxing Day led to an entertaining escapade for all of us staff and John Aspinall's guests.

Trudy
A chimpanzee who became something of a cause célèbre when her case hit the papers and TV after she came here from Mary Chipperfield. Alas, Trudy has never enjoyed a healthy life, but a comfortable existence in Hananya's family is the perfect place for her to combat her many health issues.

Tuan
A large male orang-utan exile whose amazing story in Taiwan culminated in his sanctuary at Pingtung Rescue Centre. He has had three babies at Monkey World, one with Hsiao-quai and two with RoRo.

Ursula
A female Himalayan black bear sold after the closure of Pan's Garden.